GRILL BY THE BOOK

Weekday Meals

By the Editors of Sunset Books

with special contributions by

Jerry Anne Di Vecchio
and
Betty Hughes

Sunset Books
Menlo Park, California

V-P, Sales & Marketing:
Richard A. Smeby

V-P, Editorial Director:
Bob Doyle

Production Director:
Lory Day

Art Director:
Vaskin Guiragossian

EDITORIAL STAFF FOR WEEKDAY MEALS

Coordinating Editor:
Lynne Gilberg

Research & Text:
Paula Smith Freschet

Consulting Editor:
Betty Hughes, Director, Consumer Affairs,
Weber-Stephen Products Co.

Contributing Editors:
Sandra Cameron
Barbara Sause
Cynthia Scheer

Copy Editor:
Fran Feldman

Editorial Assistant:
Jody Mitori

Photography:
Chris Shorten

Food Stylists:
Heidi Gintner
Susan Massey
Dianne Torrie
Sue White

Food Styling Assistant:
Andrea Lucich

Prop Stylist:
Laura Ferguson

Design:
Don Komai, Watermark Design

Page Layout:
Dayna Goforth

Recipe Testers:
Susan Block
Dorothy Decker
Barbara Gobar
Aileen Russell
Jean Strain
Linda Tebben

The kettle grill configuration is a registered trademark of WEBER-STEPHEN PRODUCTS CO.

The GENESIS®, PERFORMER®, SMOKEY JOE®, and GO ANYWHERE® grill configurations are trademarks of WEBER-STEPHEN PRODUCTS CO.

For more information on *Grill by the Book* or any other Sunset book, call 800-526-5111.

**A word about
our nutritional data**

For our recipes, we provide a nutritional analysis stating calorie count; percentage of calories from fat; grams of total fat and saturated fat; milligrams of cholesterol and sodium; grams of carbohydrates, fiber, and protein; and milligrams of calcium and iron. Generally, the analysis applies to a single serving, based on the number of servings given for each recipe and the amount of each ingredient. If a range is given for the number of servings and/or the amount of an ingredient, the analysis is based on the average of the figures given.

The nutritional analysis does not include optional ingredients or those for which no specific amount is stated. If an ingredient is listed with a substitution, the information was calculated using the first choice.

Contents

The Art of Grilling

Recipes

Index

Special Features

The Art of Grilling

Some folks say opposites attract, and I suppose that's how it was when Weber met Sunset. Weber is a Chicago-area company with a long tradition of forming steel into very durable barbecue grills. Sunset is a San Francisco-area company with a long tradition of forming words and photographs into informative and entertaining publications.

Weber's roots are in the Midwest, and I guess that means we really appreciate a good, thick steak and meaty ribs from the heartland. Sunset's roots are in California, where fresh Pacific seafood and an almost infinite variety of vegetables abound.

Now, even if opposites attract they must have something in common for a long-term relationship to develop.

You see, at Weber we believe you ought to buy one of our products and be pleasantly surprised that it exceeds your expectations. Sunset thinks the same way. When they write a recipe, the amount of testing they do to make sure it'll come out just so is mind-boggling.

About a year ago, Weber decided to produce a series of cookbooks to help backyard chefs have more fun with their grills. Sunset was considering a similar project. So, when we shared our mutual desire to write a series of simply great barbecue cookbooks, we decided we could make them even better if we formed a partnership.

We believe that this terrific cookbook will help you have fun with your grill, but if you have any suggestions for improvements, simply give us a call at the following number: (800) 446-1071. Your comments will help us get better at what we do, and we want to make sure you're totally satisfied with our products.

Mike Kempster

Michael Kempster, Sr.
Executive Vice President
Weber-Stephen Products Co.

A Range of Grill Options

Today's Weber® Grills come in a range of sizes, models, and prices, that offer backyard chefs a myriad of options. Before you purchase a grill, however, it's important to consider your cooking objectives. The grills described below offer a variety of convenient features that may be important to you.

No matter which Weber® model you choose, however, it's going to be a covered grill. The lid gives you the flexibility of using either the Direct or Indirect Methods of cooking. It also allows you to utilize more heat, reduces the amount of cooking time, and virtually eliminates flare-ups.

Weber® One-Touch® Charcoal Kettle

With the Weber® One-Touch® Kettle, one lever opens the vents to create the natural convection heat that helps seal in juices and flavor. The same lever also simplifies ash removal. Flip-up sides on the hinged cooking grate make it easy to add charcoal briquets while food cooks.

The kettle is available in two diameters: 18½ inches (47 cm) or 22½ inches (57 cm). Both offer plenty of cooking space.

Weber® Performer® Grill with Touch-N-Go™ Gas Ignition System

The ultimate ease in charcoal barbecuing begins with the exclusive gas ignition system on this grill, which makes quick work of lighting charcoal briquets. All you do is push a button. A high-capacity ash catcher makes cleaning easy, too. The large charcoal storage container keeps charcoal dry.

This model also has the Dual-Purpose Thermometer, the Tuck-Away™ Lid Holder, and Char-Basket™ Fuel Holders.

Weber®, Smokey Joe, and Go-Anywhere® Grills

Smaller in size than the other Weber® grills, these transportable tabletop models cook the same way as their larger counterparts. They are available in charcoal and gas models.

Weber® Genesis® 3000 Series Gas Barbecue

A convenient alternative to cooking with charcoal, this grill features specially angled Flavorizer® Bars that distribute the heat evenly and vaporize the drippings to create barbecue flavor without flare-ups. Stainless steel burners run the length of the cooking box, offering controlled, even cooking and energy efficiency.

This grill has 635 square inches (4,097 square cm) of cooking area and warming racks. Its durable porcelain-enameled cooking grate is easy to clean.

Other features include the Dual-Purpose Thermometer, weather-resistant wood work surfaces, and an easy-to-read fuel scale. Available in liquid propane and natural gas models.

Grilling Techniques

The Direct Method in a Charcoal Kettle

This grilling technique is best for relatively thin pieces of food that cook in less than 25 minutes; such as steaks, chops, burgers, boneless chicken breasts, fish fillets and steaks, and shellfish. Food is placed directly over the hot coals and must be turned once halfway through cooking time.

To prepare the grill, open all of the vents and spread charcoal briquets in a single solid layer that fills the charcoal grate. Next, mound the briquets in a pyramid-shaped pile and ignite them, keeping the lid off. When the briquets are lightly coated with gray ash (25 to 30 minutes), use long-handled tongs to spread them into a single layer again. Set the cooking grate in place and arrange the food on the grate directly over the hot coals. Place the lid on the grill, leaving all vents open, and grill as directed in your recipe, turning the food once halfway through the cooking time.

The Direct Method in a Gas Barbecue

With gas grills, use of the Direct Method is limited to preheating and searing; most of the actual cooking is done by the Indirect Method.

To preheat the grill, open the lid and check that all burner control knobs are turned to OFF and the fuel scale reads more than "E." Turn on the gas at the source. Light with the igniter switch or, if necessary, a match (see the manufacturer's directions). Check through the viewing port to be sure the burner is lit. Close the lid, turn all burners to HIGH, and preheat 10 to 15 minutes to bring the grill to 500°–550°F (260°–288°C). Then adjust the heat controls as the recipe directs and proceed to cook the food. For searing techniques, see the box at right.

Searing

Searing steaks, chops, burgers, and chicken parts that are cooked by the Indirect Method on a gas grill helps keep the meat moist by sealing in juices. The hot fat that drips from the meat creates the smoke that gives foods their distinctive barbecue flavor. A few foods cooked by the Indirect Method on a charcoal grill can also be seared. (A note with the recipe indicates if searing is recommended.)

- ■ *To sear using a gas barbecue, trim any excess fat from food. Preheat the grill as described under "Direct Method for a Gas Barbecue" (at left). Arrange the food on the preheated cooking grate and place the lid on the grill. Sear, allowing about 2 minutes for chicken parts and thinner pieces of meat, 4 minutes for thicker meat (if excess flaring occurs, turn the center burner to OFF until it subsides and then turn it to MEDIUM or LOW to complete searing).*

- ■ *Turn the food, placing it in the center of the cooking grate, and complete grilling by the Indirect Method over MEDIUM heat, turning the food once more halfway through the remaining cooking time only if directed in the recipe.*

- ■ *To sear using a charcoal kettle, ignite the briquets. Place the food at the outer edges of the cooking grate over the hot coals and sear as directed above; turn the food, placing it in the center of the cooking grate, and complete cooking by the Indirect Method as directed in the recipe.*

Indirect Cooking in a Charcoal Kettle

Use this method for thick-cut pork chops and steaks that need to cook for more than 25 minutes at lower temperatures. This technique will also be used for roasts, ribs, whole fish, turkeys and chickens. The food is not turned, and the grill must be kept covered, since every time you open the lid, heat escapes and the cooking time increases.

To set up the grill for the Indirect Method, open all vents. Position Char-Basket™ Fuel Holders or charcoal rails on either side of the charcoal grate as close as possible to the outside edges. Divide the charcoal briquets evenly and place them in the holders (see the chart below for the number to use). Ignite the briquets and, keeping the lid off, let them burn until lightly covered with gray ash (25 to 30 minutes). If necessary, use long-handled tongs to rearrange briquets so the heat will be even.

Place a foil drip pan on the charcoal grate between the baskets of coals. Put the cooking grate in place, positioning the hinged sides of the grate over the briquets so that more can be added if necessary. Arrange the food in the center of the cooking grate. Place the lid on the grill, leaving all vents open, and grill as directed. If the food is to cook for more than an hour, add briquets as indicated on the chart.

Indirect Cooking in a Gas Barbecue

Except when you are searing, the Indirect Method is always the best approach to cooking on a gas grill. Turn the food only if you are directed to do so in the recipe. The grill must be kept covered or you will have to increase the cooking time. Let foods grill for the minimum time specified in the recipe before checking for doneness.

When using the Indirect Method, preheat as directed for the Direct Method (facing page). Arrange the food in the center of the cooking grate and place the lid on the grill. For three-burner grills, set the front and back burners to MEDIUM and the center burner to OFF; for two-burner grills, turn the front and back burners to MEDIUM.

If you have another brand of grill, check your owner's manual for Indirect cooking instructions.

Quick Smoke Flavoring

When you use a covered barbecue grill, wood chips or chunks placed beneath the cooking grate can add a delicate smoked flavor. Chips are ideal for foods with shorter cooking times; chunks are best for foods that take longer. The best woods for beef are hickory, oak, mesquite, and grapevine; for pork, choose alder, apple, cherry, grapevine, hickory, or mesquite; and for lamb, try apple, cherry, or oak. You may also want to experiment with orange peels, dried corn cobs, dried fennel stocks, garlic, or woody perennial fresh herbs.

Start by soaking the wood chips or chunks in water—30 minutes for chips, one hour for chunks.

In a charcoal grill, scatter a handful or two of the wet chips right over the hot coals. With a gas grill, turn the heat to HIGH and place the chips with a little bit of water in a small foil pan directly on the heat source in the left front corner of the grill. Used as directed, a Weber® Steam-N-Chips™ Smoker makes such quick smoking a snap. Preheat the barbecue as directed and cook by the Indirect Method on MEDIUM heat.

When the wood starts smoking, begin grilling, and keep the lid on. Add more soaked chips when you no longer see smoke exiting the vents. Remember, a little smoke goes a long way—you want the flavor to complement, not overpower, the food's natural taste.

The Right Amount of Charcoal for Indirect Cooking		
Diameter of grill in inches	Briquets needed on each side for first hour	Number of briquets to add to each side every hour
26¾" (68 cm)	30	9
22½" (57 cm)	25	8
18½" (47 cm)	16	5

Fuels & Fire Starters

Charcoal briquets. Long the outdoor chef's favorite fuel, charcoal briquets are manufactured from pulverized charcoal and additives that make them easy to light. Once ignited, briquets provide good even heat, but the various brands differ somewhat in composition and density. Top-quality brands burn longer and more evenly. Store briquets in a dry place.

Self-starting briquets. Impregnated with a liquid starter, these briquets ignite with a match and heat up quickly. *Do not add self-starting briquets to an existing hot fire*—the fuel in them burns off slowly and it can spoil the flavor of the food. Always use regular briquets when additional charcoal is needed.

Liquid starter. If you use a liquid starter, be sure it's a product intended for charcoal, and follow the manufacturer's instructions closely. Let the starter soak into the coals for a few minutes; then ignite in several places. *Never* pour liquid starter on hot coals—this can cause a dangerous flare-up.

Solid starter. Solid starters such as Weber® FireStarters are safe, nontoxic, odorless cubes or sticks that light easily with a match and burn without further attention. Mound the briquets in a pyramid shape on top of the cubes, leaving a corner of the cubes exposed. Ignite the cubes, and the coals will be ready in 25 to 30 minutes.

Chimney starter. The metal cannister on this device holds a supply of charcoal briquets a few inches above the charcoal grate. Light two Weber® FireStarters or some wadded newspapers underneath the chimney, and it will bring the coals quickly to readiness.

Electric starter. Comprised of a large heating element, a handle, and an electrical cord, this device nestles in a bed of unlit briquets and ignites them when the cord is connected. After 10 minutes, remove the starter (if you leave it in too long, the heating element will burn out).

Liquid propane and natural gas. Gas barbecues use either liquid propane or gas as fuel. Liquid propane is stored in a refillable tank mounted on the barbecue grill. Expect 20 to 30 hours of use from a tank. Natural gas is piped to a grill through a permanent hookup to a gas line. *Note:* Never use one kind of fuel in a barbecue grill designed for the other.

Fire Safety

Follow the manufacturer's instructions carefully and heed the rules below to ensure safety while you grill.

■ *Never leave a hot grill unattended. Keep children and pets at a safe distance.*

■ *Never use a charcoal or gas grill indoors or in a closed garage or enclosed patio.*

■ *Do not use gasoline or other highly volatile fluids as charcoal lighters.*

■ *Do not add liquid starter to hot—or even warm—coals.*

■ *Place your grill in an open, level area away from the house, wood railings, trees, bushes, or other combustible surfaces.*

■ *Do not attempt to barbecue in high winds.*

■ *Wear an insulated, fire-retardant barbecue mitt and use long-handled tools designed for grilling. Do not wear clothing with loose, flowing sleeves.*

Grilling Guide for Poultry

Type of Poultry	Thickness or Weight	Approximate Cooking Time
BONELESS CHICKEN & TURKEY		
Place food on cooking grate, using Direct Method for a charcoal grill, Indirect Method/Medium Heat for a gas grill. Cook for time given in chart, based on medium-well 170°F (77°C), or until meat in thickest part is no longer pink; turn once halfway through cooking time.		
Chicken		
Breasts	4–5 oz (115–140 g) *each*	10 minutes
Breast cubes	1 inch (2.5 cm)	10–12 minutes
Turkey		
Tenderloins	About 6 oz (170 g) *each*	10–12 minutes
Breast slices	¼ inch (6 mm) thick	3–5 minutes
Breast cubes	1 inch (2.5 cm)	12–15 minutes
BONE-IN PIECES & WHOLE BIRDS		
Place food on cooking grate, using Indirect Method for a charcoal grill, Indirect Method/Medium Heat for a gas grill. Cook *bone-in pieces,* bone side down, for time given in chart or until no longer pink near bone; sear first, if desired. Cook *whole birds,* breast side up, for time given in chart or until an instant-read thermometer inserted in thickest part of thigh (not touching bone) registers 180°F (82°C); begin checking doneness 30 minutes before minimum cooking time.		
Chicken		
Whole	3½ –4 lbs (1.6–1.8 kg)	1–1½ hours
Halves	1½–1¾ lbs (680–795 g) *each*	50–60 minutes
Breast halves	About 8 oz (230 g) *each*	30–35 minutes
Drumsticks, thighs	4–6 oz (115–170 g) *each*	35–45 minutes
Wings	About 3 oz (85 g) *each*	30 minutes
Rock Cornish Game Hens		
Whole	1–1½ lbs (455–680 g)	45–60 minutes
Halves	8–12 oz (230–340 g) *each*	35–45 minutes
Turkey		
Whole	10–13 lbs (4.5–5.9 kg)	1½ –2¼ hours
	14–23 lbs (6.4–10.4 kg)	2½–3½ hours
Breast halves	3–3½ lbs (1.35–1.6 kg) *each*	1–1½ hours
Drumsticks, thighs	1–1½ lbs (455–680 g) *each*	55–65 minutes
Duck		
Whole	4–5 lbs (1.8–2.3 kg)	1½ –2 hours
Farm-raised, halves	12–16 oz (340–455 g) *each*	30–35 minutes
Pheasant		
Whole	2–2½ lbs (905 g–1.15 kg)	40–45 minutes

Grilling Guide for Meats

Cut of Meat	Thickness or Weight	Approximate Cooking Time

BEEF

Place steaks on cooking grate, using Direct Method for a charcoal grill, Indirect Method/Medium Heat for a gas grill. Cook for the time listed in this chart, based on medium-rare (145°F/63°C), or until desired doneness; turn once halfway through the cooking time. Sear, if desired.

Steaks (T-bone, New York, porterhouse, tenderloin, top round, sirloin, rib-eye, fillet)	1 inch (2.5 cm)	10–12 minutes
	1½ inches (3.5 cm)	14–16 minutes
	2 inches (5 cm)	20–25 minutes
Flank steak	1–2 lbs (455–905 g)	12–15 minutes
Skirt steak	¼–½ inch (6 mm–1 cm)	7–9 minutes

VEAL & LAMB

Place chops on cooking grate, using Direct Method for a charcoal grill, Indirect Method/Medium Heat for a gas grill. Cook for time given in chart, based on medium (160°F/71°C) for veal and medium-rare (145°F/63°C) for lamb, or until desired doneness; turn once halfway through cooking time. Sear, if desired.

Veal chops (rib, loin)	¾ inch (2 cm)	10–12 minutes
	1 inch (2.5 cm)	12–14 minutes
	1½ inches (3.5 cm)	16–18 minutes
Lamb chops (rib, loin, shoulder)	1 inch (2.5 cm)	10 minutes
	1½ inches (3.5 cm)	12–14 minutes

PORK

Place chops on cooking grate. On a charcoal grill, use Direct Method for ¾- to 1-inch (2- to 2.5-cm) thickness, and the Indirect Method/Medium Heat for thicker chops. On a gas grill use Indirect Method/Medium Heat for all chops. Cook for time given in chart, based on medium (160°F/71°C), or until meat near bone is no longer pink; turn once halfway through cooking time. Sear, if desired.

Chops (rib, loin, shoulder)	¾ inch (2 cm)	10–12 minutes
	1 inch (2.5 cm)	12–14 minutes
	1¼–1½ inches (3–3.5 cm)	25–35 minutes

BURGERS & SAUSAGES

Place patties or sausages on cooking grate, using Direct Method for a charcoal grill, Indirect Method/Medium Heat for a gas grill. Cook for time given in chart or until no longer pink in center and juices run clear; turn once halfway through cooking time.

Lean ground beef, lamb, pork	¾ inch (2 cm)	160°F (71°C) for medium; about 10 minutes
Lean ground chicken, turkey	¾ inch (2 cm)	165°F (74°C) for medium-well; 10–12 minutes
Sausages (uncooked), Italian (mild or hot), bratwurst, chicken, turkey, or other gourmet-type meat combinations	About 1 inch (2.5 cm) diameter	18–20 minutes

Grilling Guide for Seafood

Type of Seafood	Thickness or Weight	Approximate Cooking Time

FILLETS, STEAKS & BONELESS CUBES FOR KEBABS

Place fish on cooking grate (support less-firm fillets on heavy-duty foil), using Direct Method for a charcoal grill, Indirect Method/Medium Heat for a gas grill. Cook for time given in chart or until fish is opaque but still moist in thickest part; turn once halfway through cooking time (unless fish is on foil).

Type of Seafood	Thickness or Weight	Approximate Cooking Time
Fillets	½ inch (1 cm)	6–8 minutes
	¾ inch (2 cm)	8–10 minutes
Fillets and steaks	1 inch (2.5 cm)	10 minutes
Boneless cubes for kebabs	1 inch (2.5 cm)	8–10 minutes

WHOLE FILLETS & WHOLE FISH

Place whole fillets and whole fish, skin side down, on cooking grate (support less-firm fish on heavy-duty foil), using Indirect Method for a charcoal grill, Indirect Method/Medium Heat for a gas grill. Cook for time given in chart or until fish is opaque but still moist in thickest part.

Type of Seafood	Thickness or Weight	Approximate Cooking Time
Whole fish fillets	1½ inches (3.5 cm)	20 minutes
Whole fish	1–1½ inches (2.5–3.5 cm)	10–15 minutes
	2–2½ inches (5–6 cm)	30–35 minutes
	3 inches (8 cm)	45 minutes

SHELLFISH

Place shellfish on cooking grate, using Direct Method for a charcoal grill, Indirect Method/Medium Heat for a gas grill. Cook crab, lobster, shrimp, and scallops for time given in chart or until opaque in thickest part; turn once halfway through cooking time. Scrub and rinse live clams, mussels, and oysters; cook them until shells open; discard any that do not open.

Type of Seafood	Thickness or Weight	Approximate Cooking Time
Crab, whole (precook for 5 minutes)	About 2½ lbs (1.15 kg)	10–12 minutes
Lobster, whole (precook for 5 minutes)	About 2 lbs (905 g)	8–10 minutes
Lobster tails	8–10 oz (230–285 g)	8 minutes
Shrimp		
Large	Under 30 per lb (455 g)	4–5 minutes
Colossal (also called prawns)	10–15 per lb (455 g)	6–8 minutes
Extra-colossal (also called prawns)	Under 10 per lb (455 g)	8–10 minutes
Scallops	1–2 inches (2.5–5 cm) in diameter	5–8 minutes
Clams, hard-shell	Medium-size	5–8 minutes
Mussels	Under 12 per lb (455 g)	4–5 minutes
Oysters	Small	8 minutes

Planning Ahead

Saving time and trouble in the kitchen is a top priority for many cooks today. But while everyone strives for convenience, no one wants to give up great taste. Grilling is the perfect answer for weekday meals—even plain food tastes great when it's barbecued and there are no dirty pans to scrub. All the recipes in this book cook in an hour or less, and most are easy to prepare. Here are some time-saving tips.

■ *Plan a menu for each night of the week based on what foods are fresh and in season.*

■ *Shop for several meals at one time, so you'll have items on hand when you need them.*

■ *Make sure you have all the necessary grilling equipment.*

■ *Take advantage of make-ahead steps. Some dishes can be cooked in advance and reheated on the grill.*

■ *Marinate food the day before (if the recipe specifies); then, just before mealtime, pop the food on the grill.*

■ *Plan a time schedule for cooking a whole meal on the grill. The foods that cook the longest will be started first.*

Glossary

BASTE
Seasoned liquid brushed over food as it cooks to keep surface moist and add flavor

BUTTERFLY
To make a horizontal cut through middle of a thick piece of meat, leaving about 1 inch (2.5 cm) uncut, and then opening piece out and flattening it

CARVING BOARD
Wooden board with a well for catching juices from meat as it is being carved

CHARCOAL BRIQUETS
Compact 2-inch (5-cm) pieces of fuel made of charcoal and additives; when ignited, they provide even heat for cooking

CHAR-BASKET™ FUEL HOLDERS
Hold charcoal against sides of grill to provide a larger cooking area when Indirect Method is used; charcoal rails serve the same function

COOKING GRATE
Metal grill on which food is cooked; hinged sides facilitate addition of charcoal briquets

DEGLAZE
To loosen drippings on bottom of a roasting or frying pan by stirring in wine, stock, or another liquid

DIRECT METHOD
Grilling technique, used for small or thin cuts of meat and other foods that cook in less than 25 minutes; the food is cooked directly over heat source and turned once halfway through grilling time; on a gas grill, used only for preheating and searing

DRY RUB
Highly concentrated blend of herbs and spices that is rubbed all over food before cooking to impart flavor

DRIP PAN
Foil pan placed beneath food to catch melted fat and juices when food is cooked by Indirect Method

GLAZE
To coat with a baste or sauce, so as to give a sheen to cooked food

GRIDDLE
Heavy, flat pan with a metal handle usually made of cast iron and used to cook breakfast fare, fajitas, or grilled sandwiches

GRILL BRUSH
Stiff brass bristle brush used for removing stubborn food residue from the cooking grate

GRILLING
Cooking food on a metal grate over a heat source (charcoal, gas, or electric coil)

INDIRECT METHOD
Grilling technique, used primarily for larger cuts of meat and other foods that require cooking times longer than 25 minutes; food is cooked by reflected heat (not directly above heat source), sealing in juices and eliminating the need for turning; this method can only be used with a covered grill

INSTANT-READ THERMOMETER
Type of meat thermometer that registers the internal temperature of food within seconds of being inserted; they are not safe for use in the oven

MARINADE
Seasoned liquid (usually containing an acidic ingredient, such as vinegar, wine, or citrus juice) in which food soaks, tenderizing it and enhancing flavor

SEAR
To brown meat directly above heat source at a high temperature, for just a brief time, to seal in juices

SKEWER
Thin metal or bamboo sticks of various lengths on which pieces of meat, poultry, fish, or vegetables are secured prior to grilling

SPATULA
Flat, thin tool used to turn and lift foods on the grill

TONGS
Tool used to grasp and turn foods; usually made of metal with two pieces joined at one end

WOOD CHIPS
Small chips of dried, fragrant hardwoods used to impart a smoky flavor to foods

WOOD CHUNKS
Chunks of dried, fragrant hardwoods used either as a fuel or to add smoky flavor to foods as they cook

ZEST
Thin, outermost layer of peel (colored part only) of citrus fruits

Recipes

Thai Garlic Beef

As Thai food goes, this dish is relatively tame in its spiciness. As such, it's an excellent choice for introducing your family to the captivating flavors of Thai cooking. The cucumber-and-papaya relish is a delightful counterpoint to the garlicky beef.

Charcoal	Direct
Gas	Indirect/Medium Heat
Grilling time	10–12 minutes

	Thai Relish (see below)
6	cloves garlic, minced or pressed
⅓	cup (80 ml) finely chopped cilantro
2	tablespoons lime juice
1	tablespoon coarsely ground pepper
1	boneless beef top sirloin steak, about 1½ pounds (680 g), cut about 1 inch (2.5 cm) thick, trimmed of fat
	Tomato wedges
	Lime wedges
	Cilantro sprigs
	Salt

Thai Relish

1	cup (240 ml) *each* finely diced cucumber and papaya
¼	cup (60 ml) thinly sliced green onions
2	tablespoons lime juice
¼	teaspoon crushed red pepper flakes
2	cloves garlic, minced or pressed

Lowfat

In a large bowl, combine ingredients for Thai Relish. Cover and refrigerate until ready to use or for up to 4 hours.

In a small bowl, combine garlic, chopped cilantro, lime juice, and pepper. Pat mixture all over steak. Arrange steak on cooking grate. Place lid on grill. Cook, turning once halfway through cooking time, until meat is done to your liking (12 to 15 minutes for medium-rare; cut to test).

Transfer beef to a platter and slice thinly across grain. Garnish with tomato wedges, lime wedges, and cilantro sprigs. Serve with relish. Season to taste with salt.

MAKES 6 SERVINGS.

Per serving: 154 calories (29% from fat), 5 g total fat (2 g saturated fat), 59 mg cholesterol, 49 mg sodium, 6 g carbohydrates, 1 g fiber, 21 g protein, 32 mg calcium, 3 mg iron

Beef Brisket with Double-duty Marinade

The brisket marinates for up to two days before it's grilled. The marinade is then used as the base for a thickened, mustard-flavored sauce that is served with the beef.

Charcoal	Indirect
Gas	Indirect/Medium Heat Searing (optional) see page 6
Marinating time	1–2 days
Grilling time	About 1 hour

1   center-cut beef brisket, about 5 pounds (2.3 kg), cut about 2 inches (5 cm) thick, trimmed of fat

1   small onion, minced

½   cup (120 ml) Worcestershire

2   tablespoons *each* soy sauce and liquid smoke

½   teaspoon ground red pepper (cayenne)

½   cup (120 ml)) butter or margarine

½   cup (120 ml) *each* catsup and red wine vinegar

1   teaspoon dried mustard

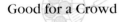

Good for a Crowd

Make a horizontal cut through middle of meat, leaving about 1 inch (2.5 cm) uncut, and lay meat open. With your palms, press meat to flatten it evenly.

Combine onion, Worcestershire, soy sauce, liquid smoke, and ground red pepper in a large heavy-duty plastic food bag. Add meat and seal bag securely. Rotate bag to distribute marinade and set in a shallow pan. Refrigerate until next day or for up to 2 days, turning bag occasionally.

Remove meat from bag and drain; pour marinade into a 1- to 2-quart (950-ml to 1.9-liter) pan. Add butter, catsup, vinegar, and mustard to marinade. Boil over high heat, stirring, until reduced to about 1½ cups/360 ml (about 15 minutes). Arrange meat, open in butterfly position, in center of cooking grate. Place lid on grill. Cook, brushing occasionally with marinade mixture, until an instant-read thermometer inserted in thickest part of meat registers 145°F (63°C) for medium-rare (about 1 hour).

Cut meat across grain into thin, slanting slices. Serve with any remaining marinade.

MAKES 12 SERVINGS.

Per serving: 329 calories (56% from fat), 20 g total fat (9 g saturated fat), 110 mg cholesterol, 546 mg sodium, 6 g carbohydrates, 0 g fiber, 30 g protein, 13 mg calcium, 3 mg iron

Skewered Beef & Corn

Pineapple juice and red wine combine in a marinade for skewers of beef, corn on the cob, bell peppers, onions, and fresh pineapple. Start marinating the meat in the morning. In the evening, assemble the skewers, and dinner will be ready in no time.

Charcoal	Direct
Gas	Indirect/Medium Heat
Marinating time	6 hours or until next day
Grilling time	About 15 minutes

Pineapple-Wine Marinade (see below)

4 pounds (1.8 kg) boneless chuck roast, trimmed of fat, cut into about 1½-inch (3.5-cm) cubes

¼ cup (60 ml) butter or margarine, melted

¼ cup (60 ml) salad oil

5 medium-size ears corn, husked and cut into about 2-inch (5-cm) lengths

3 medium-size green bell peppers, cut into about 1½-inch (3.5-cm) squares

2 large red onions, cut into about 1½-inch (3.5-cm) chunks

1 medium-size pineapple, peeled, cored, and cut into about 1½-inch (3.5-cm) cubes

Pineapple-Wine Marinade

1½ cups (360 ml) *each* pineapple juice and dry red wine

1½ tablespoons minced onion

1½ teaspoons *each* Worcestershire and dried thyme

¾ teaspoon dried mustard

¼ cup (60 ml) firmly packed brown sugar

¼ teaspoon pepper

2 cloves garlic, minced or pressed

In a large bowl, combine ingredients for Pineapple-Wine Marinade. Set aside ⅓ cup (80 ml) of the marinade; pour remaining marinade into a large heavy-duty plastic food bag or nonreactive bowl. Add meat and seal bag (or cover bowl). Rotate bag to distribute marinade and place in a shallow pan. Refrigerate for at least 6 hours or until next day, turning meat occasionally.

In a small bowl, combine butter, oil, and reserved marinade; set aside. Remove meat from bag and drain, discarding marinade in bag. On 8 long metal skewers, thread meat with corn (through cob), bell peppers, onions, and pineapple. Brush all over with butter mixture.

Arrange skewers on cooking grate. Place lid on grill. Cook, turning once and brushing with remaining butter mixture halfway through cooking time, until meat is done to your liking (about 15 minutes for medium-rare; cut to test). Transfer skewers to individual plates.

MAKES 8 SERVINGS.

Per serving: 749 calories (53% from fat), 44 g total fat (17 g saturated fat), 159 mg cholesterol, 148 mg sodium, 41 g carbohydrates, 5 g fiber, 46 g protein, 63 mg calcium, 6 mg iron

Skewer Savvy

You can prepare a delicious meal on the grill in a matter of minutes simply by pulling together items you already have on hand. Skewering varied combinations of food allows you to create a new and different meal each time. And using skewers means no more rescuing your dinner from the coals!

In a charcoal kettle, cook by the Direct Method, using about three-quarters the usual number of briquets; one sparse layer of coals is just right.

In a gas barbecue, use the Indirect Method/Medium Heat. Turn the skewers once halfway through the cooking time.

Here are some helpful hints for skewering:

- *Use parallel skewers (or a double-pronged skewer) to keep food, particularly vegetables and fruit, from spinning or flopping.*

- *To avoid splitting crisp or firm vegetables and fruit, use slender, sharply pointed skewers. Soak wooden skewers in water for 30 minutes before skewering the food to prevent the wood from charring.*

- *Always wear insulated, fire-retardant barbecue mitts when you turn skewers or remove them from the grill. Metal skewers become very hot.*

- *Beef sirloin, lean pork, lamb, and chicken are all good choices (the meat must be boneless). Choose fish with firm, dense flesh or use large scallops or shelled, deveined shrimp. Cut into 1-inch (2.5 cm) cubes.*

- *Good vegetables and fruit for skewering are listed on pages 38–39. Cut into 1-inch chunks or wedges. Parboil potatoes just until tender before threading them onto skewers. Grill vegetables and fruit just until tender when pierced.*

Beef Pocket Sandwiches

Thin strips of grilled beef retain their wavy shapes even after they're removed from the skewers. Combined with squares of grilled red pepper, they make a fun filling for these meal-in-a-pocket sandwiches.

Charcoal	Direct
Gas	Indirect/Medium Heat
Marinating time	30 minutes or until next day
Grilling time	About 4 minutes

1   boneless beef top sirloin steak, about 1½ pounds (680 g), cut about 1 inch (2.5 cm) thick, trimmed of fat

1   large clove garlic

½   small onion, cut into chunks

2   tablespoons *each* sugar, salad oil, and lemon juice

⅓   cup (80 ml) reduced-sodium soy sauce

2   large red bell peppers, cut into about 1½-inch (3.5-cm) squares

6   pita breads, about 6 inches (15 cm) in diameter, cut in half

2   cups (470 ml) lightly packed cilantro sprigs, rinsed and crisped

Very Easy

Cut beef into long slices about ¼ inch (6 mm) thick.

In a blender or food processor, whirl garlic, onion, sugar, oil, lemon juice, soy sauce, and 2 tablespoons water until smooth. Pour into a large heavy-duty plastic food bag or nonreactive bowl. Add beef and bell peppers and seal bag (or cover bowl). Rotate bag to distribute marinade and place in a shallow pan. Refrigerate for at least 30 minutes or until next day, turning food occasionally.

Remove beef and bell peppers from bag and drain, reserving marinade. On skewers, thread beef strips alternately with bell peppers (to thread beef, pierce an end of strip with skewer and then fold back and forth several times, piercing each time). Arrange skewers on cooking grate. Place lid on grill. Cook, turning once and brushing with reserved marinade halfway through cooking time, until beef is done to your liking (about 4 minutes for medium-rare; cut to test).

Fill pita halves with beef, bell peppers, and cilantro.

MAKES 6 SERVINGS.

Per serving: .387 calories (24% from fat), 10 g total fat (3 g saturated fat), 59 mg cholesterol, 898 mg sodium, 45 g carbohydrates, 2 g fiber, 27 g protein, 79 mg calcium, 5 mg iron

Tangy Flank Steak Sandwiches

*Toasted French rolls filled with thinly sliced marinated steak,
lettuce, onion, and tomato will satisfy even the healthiest of appetites. Kids will love shelling the
peas that grill in their pods alongside the meat.*

Charcoal	Direct
Gas	Indirect/Medium Heat
Marinating time	1 hour or until next day
Grilling time	12–15 minutes

²⁄₃   cup (160 ml) catsup

¹⁄₃   cup (80 ml) dry red wine
     or lemon juice

1   tablespoon minced fresh
     basil or 1 teaspoon dried
     basil

2   teaspoons Worcestershire

1   teaspoon celery seeds

2   bay leaves

¹⁄₂   teaspoon pepper

1   flank steak, about 1½
     pounds (680 g), about
     1 inch (2.5 cm) thick,
     trimmed of fat

2   to 2½ pounds (905 g to
     1.15 kg) unshelled peas,
     rinsed

     Salt

     Lettuce leaves, rinsed
     and crisped

     Thinly sliced white onion
     or green bell pepper

     Thinly sliced tomato

4   or 5 French rolls, split
     and toasted

In a 1- to 1½-quart (950-ml to 1.4-liter) pan, combine catsup, wine, basil, Worcestershire, celery seeds, bay leaves, pepper, and ½ cup (120 ml) water. Simmer over medium heat, stirring occasionally, for 10 minutes; let cool.

Using a sharp knife, make light diagonal cuts across both sides of steak about 1 inch (2.5 cm) apart, forming a diamond pattern. Place meat in a large heavy-duty plastic food bag. Pour marinade over meat and seal bag securely. Rotate bag to distribute marinade and place in a shallow pan. Refrigerate for at least 1 hour or until next day, turning bag occasionally.

Divide peas into 4 or 5 portions, placing each on a piece of heavy-duty foil. Sprinkle lightly with salt and 1 tablespoon water; wrap tightly.

Remove meat from bag and drain; pour marinade from bag into a 1- to 1½-quart (950-ml to 1.4-liter) metal-handled pan and set aside. Arrange meat and foil packets on cooking grate. Place lid on grill. Cook, turning food once halfway through cooking time, until meat is done to your liking and peas are tender (10 to 15 minutes for peas, 12 to 15 minutes for medium-rare steak; cut meat to test). About 5 minutes before meat is done, set pan with marinade on cooking grate. Heat until simmering (about 5 minutes).

Cut meat diagonally across grain into thin slices. Place lettuce, onion, and tomato on rolls; top with meat. Place pea packets alongside sandwiches. Serve with marinade.

MAKES 4 OR 5 SERVINGS.

Per serving: 544 calories (24% from fat), 14 g total fat (6 g saturated fat), 68 mg cholesterol, 1045 mg sodium, 62 g carbohydrates, 9 g fiber, 39 g protein, 210 mg calcium, 6 mg iron

Hamburgers & Corn with Jerk Sauce

Jalapeño chiles deliver the heat for this appetizing meal; authentic Jamaican flavor comes from the allspice and nutmeg. Both the grilled corn and the burgers benefit from being slathered with the tasty jerk sauce.

Charcoal	Direct
Gas	Indirect/Medium Heat
Grilling time	15–20 minutes

Jerk Sauce (see below)

4	large ears corn, unhusked
1	to 1½ pounds (455 to 680 g) lean ground beef
4	hamburger buns, split and toasted
	Lettuce leaves, rinsed and crisped
	Mayonnaise
	Salt

Jerk Sauce

1	cup (240 ml) chopped green onions
¼	cup (60 ml) lime juice
2	tablespoons *each* dark molasses, soy sauce, and chopped fresh ginger
2	cloves garlic
2	fresh jalapeño chiles, seeded and chopped
½	teaspoon ground cinnamon
¼	teaspoon *each* ground allspice and ground nutmeg

In a blender or food processor, combine ingredients for Jerk Sauce. Whirl until finely minced.

Gently pull husks back from corn without tearing from cob. Remove and discard silk. Rinse corn and pat dry. Smear about 1 tablespoon of the sauce over each ear. Lay husks back around corn; tie near top with cotton string to enclose. Shape meat into 4 equal-size patties, each about ¾ inch (2 cm) thick. If made ahead, wrap and refrigerate corn and beef patties separately for up to 2 hours.

Arrange corn on cooking grate. Place lid on grill. Cook, turning corn occasionally to keep husks from burning, until kernels are very hot (15 to 20 minutes). About 10 minutes before corn is done, arrange meat on grate. Place lid on grill. Cook, turning patties once halfway through cooking time (about 10 minutes for medium; cut to test).

Transfer patties to hamburger buns. Top with lettuce, sauce, and mayonnaise. Husk corn and serve with more sauce. Season to taste with salt.

MAKES 4 SERVINGS.

Per serving: 570 calories (35% from fat), 23 g total fat (8 g saturated fat), 88 mg cholesterol, 868 mg sodium, 61 g carbohydrates, 6 g fiber, 34 g protein, 192 mg calcium, 7 mg iron

Internal Temperatures for Safe Cooking

The USDA recommendation is that ground meat be cooked to 160°F (71°C) in center of patties or until no longer pink and the juices run clear. Ground poultry should be cooked to 165°F (74°C).

GRILL BY THE BOOK
T I P

When grilling corn without a sauce, leave cobs in their husks, soak in cold water about 30 minutes; then grill. Peel back husks—silk will pull away cleanly.

Rubs & Bastes for Meats

Plain grilled meats are often delicious, but today's diners want variety as well as good taste. Here is a selection of flavored dry rubs, bastes, and butters to enhance all kinds of meats. Or try them on corn and potatoes before grilling. Experiment with some of your own combinations as well—the possibilities are endless. For rubs and bastes that work especially well with poultry and fish, see page 48.

Chili Salt

1¾ teaspoons chili powder

¾ teaspoon salt

In a small bowl, combine chili powder and salt. Sprinkle mixture all over meat before cooking.

MAKES 2½ TEASPOONS, ENOUGH FOR ABOUT 4 SERVINGS OF MEAT.

Per serving: 3 calories (36% from fat), 0 g total fat (0 g saturated fat), 0 mg cholesterol, 423 mg sodium, 1 g carbohydrates, 0 g fiber, 0 g protein, 6 mg calcium, 0 mg iron

Curry Paste

1 tablespoon butter or margarine

1 tablespoon curry powder

¾ teaspoon salt

In an 8- to 10-inch (20- to 25-cm) frying pan, melt butter over medium-high heat. Stir in curry powder and salt and let bubble for 30 seconds. Brush curry mixture all over meat before cooking.

MAKES ABOUT 1½ TABLESPOONS, ENOUGH FOR ABOUT 8 SERVINGS OF MEAT.

Per serving: 15 calories (86% from fat), 2 g total fat (1 g saturated fat), 4 mg cholesterol, 221 mg sodium, 0 g carbohydrates, 0 g fiber, 0 g protein, 6 mg calcium, 0 mg iron

Pepper & Spice Rub

1 tablespoon *each* whole juniper berries, whole black peppercorns, and whole allspice

In a blender or food processor, combine juniper berries, peppercorns, and allspice. Whirl until coarsely ground. Or mince berries, and crush pepper and allspice with a mortar and pestle; mix together. Pat pepper mixture firmly all over meat before cooking.

MAKES ABOUT 3 TABLESPOONS, ENOUGH FOR ABOUT 8 SERVINGS OF MEAT.

Per serving: 6 calories (11% from fat), 0 g total fat (0 g saturated fat), 0 mg cholesterol, 1 mg sodium, 2 g carbohydrates, 0 g fiber, 0 g protein, 12 mg calcium, 1 mg iron

Herb & Mustard Baste

3 tablespoons *each* olive oil and red wine vinegar

1 tablespoon Dijon mustard

1 clove garlic, minced or pressed

¼ teaspoon pepper

2 tablespoons minced fresh tarragon or 1 tablespoon *each* minced fresh thyme and fresh rosemary

In a small bowl, combine oil, vinegar, mustard, garlic, pepper, and tarragon. Whisk until blended. Brush mixture all over meat while it cooks.

MAKES ABOUT ½ CUP (120 ML), ENOUGH FOR ABOUT 8 SERVINGS OF MEAT.

Per serving: 49 calories (95% from fat), 5 g total fat (1 g saturated fat), 0 mg cholesterol, 45 mg sodium, 0 g carbohydrates, 0 g fiber, 0 g protein, 4 mg calcium, 0 mg iron

Garlic & Herb Rub

1   large head garlic

6   bay leaves

Separate garlic cloves; peel cloves. In a food processor or blender, whirl garlic until puréed. Pat garlic all over meat before cooking. Press bay leaves into garlic.

MAKES ABOUT ⅓ CUP (80 ML), ENOUGH FOR ABOUT 6 SERVINGS OF MEAT.

Per serving: 28 calories (5% from fat), 0 g total fat (0 g saturated fat), 0 mg cholesterol, 3 mg sodium, 6 g carbohydrates, 0 g fiber, 1 g protein, 39 mg calcium, 1 mg iron

Blue Cheese Butter for Beef & Lamb

4   ounces (115 g) double or triple crème blue-veined cheese, such as cambozola or Blue Castello, at room temperature

Cut cheese into 6 equal-size pieces. Place a piece on each serving of hot cooked meat.

MAKES 4 OUNCES (115 G), ENOUGH FOR ABOUT 6 SERVINGS OF MEAT.

Per serving: 87 calories (87% from fat), 8 g total fat (5 g saturated fat), 27 mg cholesterol, 120 mg sodium, 0 g carbohydrates, 0 g fiber, 3 g protein, 133 mg calcium, 0 mg iron

Tapenade

½   cup (120 ml) pitted ripe olives or oil-cured olives (cut meat from pits)

¼   cup (60 ml) drained capers

2   teaspoons Dijon mustard

5   canned anchovy fillets, drained

¼   teaspoon *each* cracked bay leaves and dried thyme

1   large clove garlic, minced or pressed

In a food processor or blender, combine olives, capers, mustard, anchovies, bay leaves, thyme, and garlic. Whirl until finely chopped but not puréed. Pat mixture all over meat before cooking.

MAKES ABOUT ½ CUP (120 ML), ENOUGH FOR 4 HEAVILY SEASONED OR 8 LIGHTLY SEASONED SERVINGS OF MEAT.

Per serving: 34 calories (62% from fat), 2 g total fat (0 g saturated fat), 3 mg cholesterol, 611 mg sodium, 1 g carbohydrates, 1 g fiber, 2 g protein, 30 mg calcium, 1 mg iron

Old-fashioned Barbecue Sauce

2   tablespoons salad oil

1   clove garlic, minced or pressed

1   can, about 6 ounces (170 g), tomato paste

½   cup (120 ml) light molasses

¼   cup (60 ml) *each* prepared mustard and soy sauce

3   tablespoons Worcestershire

2   tablespoons red wine vinegar

2   teaspoons ground sage

1   to 3 teaspoons liquid hot pepper seasoning

½   to 1 teaspoon pepper

     Salt

Heat oil in a 2- to 3-quart (1.9- to 2.8-liter) pan over low heat. Add garlic and cook, stirring, until golden (about 5 minutes). Stir in tomato paste, molasses, mustard, soy sauce, Worcestershire, vinegar, sage, and hot pepper seasoning and pepper to taste. Simmer until flavors are blended (about 10 minutes). Season to taste with salt. Brush sauce all over meat while it cooks.

MAKES ABOUT 2 CUPS (470 ML).

Per ¼ cup (60 ml): 121 calories (28% from fat), 4 g total fat (1 g saturated fat), 0 mg cholesterol, 883 mg sodium, 21 g carbohydrates, 1 g fiber, 2 g protein, 62 mg calcium, 2 mg iron

Fajita Nachos

Cooking with beer is great, especially if you're cooking for a crowd. A little brew goes in the marinade for this beef; a little more gives muscle to the mashed pinto beans. The beans and onions can be prepared a day ahead.

Charcoal	Direct
Gas	Indirect/Medium Heat Searing (optional) see page 6
Marinating time	2 hours or until next day
Grilling time	7–9 minutes

¼   cup (60 ml) *each* lime juice and olive oil

1½   cups (360 ml) beer

2   cloves garlic, minced or pressed

1   teaspoon *each* ground coriander and ground cumin

1   fresh jalapeño chile, seeded and minced

1   pound (455 g) beef skirt or flank steak, trimmed of fat

2   cans, about 15 ounces (425 g) *each*, pinto beans, drained

Salt

2   medium-size onions, chopped

Lime Salsa (see below)

1   cup (240 ml) shredded Cheddar cheese

Guacamole (purchased or homemade)

About 2 quarts (1.9 liters) tortilla chips

Lime Salsa

1   large yellow or red tomato, finely diced

2   large tomatillos, husks removed, finely diced

¼   cup (60 ml) finely diced red bell pepper

2   tablespoons minced red onion

1   teaspoon grated lime zest

1   tablespoon lime juice

Combine the ¼ cup (60 ml) lime juice, 3 tablespoons of the oil, ½ cup (120 ml) of the beer, garlic, coriander, cumin, and chile in a large heavy-duty plastic food bag. Set aside 3 tablespoons of the marinade. Add steak to bag and seal securely. Rotate bag to distribute marinade and place in a shallow pan. Refrigerate for at least 2 hours or until next day, turning bag occasionally.

Meanwhile, combine reserved marinade, beans, and remaining beer in a 2- to 3-quart (1.9- to 2.8-liter) pan. Cook over medium heat, stirring and mashing beans coarsely with back of a spoon or a potato masher, until slightly thickened (15 to 20 minutes). Season to taste with salt. Heat remaining oil in a wide frying pan over medium heat. Add onions and cook, partially covered and stirring often, until very soft and golden brown (15 to 20 minutes). If made ahead, cover beans and onions separately and refrigerate until next day; reheat beans before using.

Combine ingredients for Lime Salsa in a bowl. Cover and refrigerate until ready to use or for up to 4 hours. Remove meat from bag and drain, discarding marinade. Arrange steak on cooking grate. Place lid on grill. Cook, turning once halfway through cooking time, until meat is done to your liking (for medium-rare: 7 to 9 minutes for skirt steak, 12 to 15 minutes for flank steak; cut to test). Thinly slice meat across grain; then cut into bite-size pieces.

Spread beans into about a 10-inch (25-cm) circle in a large pizza or other metal pan. Top with onions, steak, and cheese. Set pan on cooking grate. Place lid on grill. Cook until cheese is melted (about 5 minutes). Top with guacamole and some of the salsa. Tuck some of the tortilla chips around edges. Serve with remaining chips and salsa.

MAKES 6 MAIN-COURSE SERVINGS.

Per serving: 735 calories (48% from fat), 39 g total fat (11 g saturated fat), 57 mg cholesterol, 726 mg sodium, 64 g carbohydrates, 10 g fiber, 31 g protein, 290 mg calcium, 5 mg iron

Honey-Mustard Ribs & Wings

Ribs and wings put finger-licking fun into a weekday dinner. Marinate them overnight in plastic bags; then toss them on the grill when you're ready for dinner.

Charcoal	Indirect
Gas	Indirect/Medium Heat Searing (optional) see page 6
Marinating time	4 hours or until next day
Grilling time	About 30 minutes

1   cup (240 ml) Dijon mustard

1   cup (240 ml) dry white wine or chicken broth

2   tablespoons *each* olive oil and honey

1   tablespoon minced fresh tarragon or 2 teaspoons dried tarragon

2   cloves garlic, minced or pressed

3   pounds (1.35 kg) chicken wings

3   pounds (1.35 kg) beef ribs trimmed of fat, cut into separate ribs

Very Easy

In a small bowl, combine mustard, wine, oil, honey, tarragon, and garlic. Rinse chicken and pat dry. Place wings and ribs in separate large heavy-duty plastic food bags. Pour half the marinade into each bag and seal securely. Rotate bags to distribute marinade and place in a shallow pan. Refrigerate for at least 4 hours or until next day, turning bags occasionally.

Remove food from bags and drain, reserving marinade. Arrange ribs and wings, overlapping if necessary, in center of cooking grate. Place lid on grill. Cook, brushing once with reserved marinade halfway through cooking time, until ribs are browned but still slightly pink near bone and wings are browned and no longer pink near bone (20 to 25 minutes for medium-rare ribs, about 30 minutes for wings; cut to test).

MAKES 6 SERVINGS.

Per serving: 631 calories (68% from fat), 45 g total fat (15 g saturated fat), 146 mg cholesterol, 607 mg sodium, 3 g carbohydrates, 0 g fiber, 43 g protein, 29 mg calcium, 3 mg iron

Best-ever Chinese Ribs

*To make a simple and attractive side dish for these easy ribs,
skewer squares of red, green, and yellow bell peppers. Brush the skewered vegetables with the
marinade and grill them with the ribs during the last 15 minutes of cooking.*

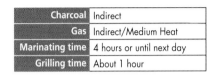

Charcoal	Indirect
Gas	Indirect/Medium Heat
Marinating time	4 hours or until next day
Grilling time	About 1 hour

¾ cup (150 g) sugar

½ cup (120 ml) soy sauce

3 tablespoons hoisin sauce

2 tablespoons dry sherry

1 tablespoon minced fresh ginger

2 cloves garlic, minced or pressed

3 to 4 pounds (1.35 to 1.8 kg) pork baby back ribs or pork spareribs (have spareribs sawn in half crosswise), trimmed of fat

Very Easy

Combine sugar, soy sauce, hoisin, sherry, ginger, and garlic in a 12- by 17-inch (30- by 43-cm) pan. Add ribs and coat with marinade. Cover and refrigerate for at least 4 hours or until next day, turning ribs occasionally.

Remove ribs from pan and drain, reserving marinade. Arrange ribs, meat side up, in center of cooking grate. Place lid on grill. Cook until ribs are well browned and meat near bone is no longer pink (about 1 hour; cut to test). About 15 minutes before ribs are done, begin brushing occasionally with reserved marinade.

Cut ribs between bones into serving-size portions.

MAKES 3 OR 4 SERVINGS.

Per serving: 915 calories (57% from fat), 57 g total fat (21 g saturated fat), 226 mg cholesterol, 2489 mg sodium, 49 g carbohydrates, 0 g fiber, 49 g protein, 96 mg calcium, 3 mg iron

Sweet & Spicy Chicken & Ribs

This tomato-based barbecue sauce is likely to become a favorite in your household. Here, it's enjoyed two ways—with both chicken and ribs.

Charcoal	Indirect
Gas	Indirect/Medium Heat
Marinating time	3 hours or until next day
Grilling time	About 1 hour

- 1   can, about 8 ounces (230 g), tomato sauce
- 1   can, about 6 ounces (170 g), tomato paste
- ⅓   cup (80 ml) dry sherry
- ¼   cup (60 ml) *each* firmly packed brown sugar and honey
- 2   tablespoons Worcestershire
- 1   tablespoon dried mustard
- ½   cup (120 ml) minced onion
- 2   cloves garlic, minced or pressed
- 1   teaspoon ground ginger
- ½   teaspoon pepper
- 1½   cups orange juice
- 1   chicken, about 3½ pounds (1.6 kg), cut up
- 3   pounds (1.35 kg) lean pork spareribs, trimmed of fat

In a large bowl, combine tomato sauce, tomato paste, sherry, sugar, honey, Worcestershire, mustard, onion, garlic, ginger, pepper, and orange juice.

Remove and discard excess fat from chicken. Rinse and pat dry. Place in a large heavy-duty plastic food bag and pour in 2½ cups (590 ml) of the marinade. Place ribs in another bag; pour in remaining marinade. Seal bags securely. Rotate bags to distribute marinade and place in a shallow pan. Refrigerate for at least 3 hours or until next day, turning bags occasionally.

Remove ribs and chicken from bags and drain, reserving marinade. Arrange ribs in center of cooking grate. Place lid on grill. Cook for 15 minutes. Add chicken and continue to cook until meat is well browned and no longer pink near bone (about 45 more minutes; cut to test). About 20 minutes before meat is done, begin brushing occasionally with reserved marinade.

Transfer ribs to a carving board and cut between ribs.

Makes 6 servings.

Per serving: 805 calories (50% from fat), 43 g total fat (14 g saturated fat), 210 mg cholesterol, 692 mg sodium, 39 g carbohydrates, 2 g fiber, 60 g protein, 97 mg calcium, 5 mg iron

GRILL BY THE BOOK
TIP

Cleanup is easy if you marinate your food in heavy-duty plastic food bags placed in a shallow pan or dish.

Glazed Pork Chops

Try these spicy chops with simple skewers of grilled corn, onion, and bell peppers.
Or, turn to pages 38–39 for other ideas.

Charcoal	Direct
Gas	Indirect/Medium Heat
Grilling time	12–14 minutes

½ cup (120 ml) hot-seasoned catsup

1 tablespoon *each* honey and lime juice

¼ teaspoon ground red pepper (cayenne)

6 center-cut pork chops, about 2½ pounds (1.15 kg) *total*, cut about 1 inch (2.5 cm) thick, trimmed of fat

2 large lemons, cut into wedges

Lowfat

In a small bowl, combine catsup, honey, lime juice, and ground red pepper. Brush tops of chops thickly with sauce.

Arrange chops on cooking grate. Place lid on grill. Cook, turning once and brushing tops thickly with remaining sauce halfway through cooking time, until meat near bone is no longer pink (12 to 14 minutes; cut to test). Transfer chops to a platter or individual plates and serve with lemon wedges to squeeze over meat.

MAKES 4 TO 6 SERVINGS.

Per serving: 232 calories (29% from fat), 8 g total fat (3 g saturated fat), 76 mg cholesterol, 298 mg sodium, 13 g carbohydrates, 0 g fiber, 29 g protein, 57 mg calcium, 1 mg iron

Pork Tenderloin Surprise Package

Don't be surprised if you're asked to make this dish time and again. Elegant medallions of pork tenderloin are topped with onion, tomato, and bell pepper; then wrapped in bacon. The last-minute finishing touch is a slice of melted provolone cheese.

Charcoal	Indirect
Gas	Indirect/Medium Heat
Grilling time	40–50 minutes

12   thick-cut slices bacon, about 12 ounces (340 g) *total*

1½   pounds (680 g) pork tenderloin, cut into 6 slices about 1½ inches (3.5 cm) thick

       Freshly ground pepper

1   medium-size onion, cut into 6 slices about ¼ inch (6 mm) thick

1   large tomato, cut into 6 slices about ½ inch (1 cm) thick

1   medium-size yellow or green bell pepper, cut into 6 pieces

3   ounces (85 g) provolone cheese, cut into 6 thin slices

For each package, cross 2 bacon slices and place a pork slice in center where bacon slices cross. Sprinkle meat lightly with pepper. Top pork with an onion slice, a tomato slice, and a bell pepper piece. Bring bacon slices around stack and secure on top with a wooden pick. Repeat to assemble remaining packages.

Arrange packages in center of cooking grate. Place lid on grill. Cook until an instant-read thermometer inserted in thickest part of meat registers 160°F (71°C) and meat in center is no longer pink (40 to 50 minutes for medium; cut to test). About 5 minutes before meat is done, top each package with a slice of cheese.

MAKES 6 SERVINGS.

Per serving: 326 calories (51% from fat), 18 g total fat (7 g saturated fat), 98 mg cholesterol, 440 mg sodium, 7 g carbohydrates, 2 g fiber, 33 g protein, 125 mg calcium, 2 mg iron

Pork Loin on Rye with Apple Chutney

*Try these terrific sandwiches when you need a casual lunch or dinner for a small group.
The chutney will keep for up to 3 weeks, so you can do much of the work
for this meal in advance.*

Charcoal	Indirect
Gas	Indirect/Medium Heat
Marinating time	2 hours or until next day
Grilling time	About 1 hour

	Apple Chutney (see below)
1	tablespoon honey
1	tablespoon minced fresh sage leaves or 1 teaspoon dried sage
1	clove garlic, minced or pressed
1	teaspoon crushed juniper berries
¼	teaspoon pepper
1	boned, rolled, and tied center-cut pork loin, 2 to 2¼ pounds (905 g to 1.02 kg)
12	slices caraway-rye bread
	Coarse-grained mustard
6	leaves butter lettuce

Apple Chutney

2	large Newtown pippin apples, peeled, cored, and chopped
½	small onion, chopped
½	lemon, unpeeled, seeded and finely chopped
½	small red bell pepper, chopped
2	tablespoons minced fresh ginger
1	clove garlic, minced or pressed
⅓	cup (80 ml) apple cider vinegar
⅔	cup (160 ml) firmly packed light brown sugar
⅛	teaspoon ground red pepper (cayenne)
½	teaspoon salt

To prepare Apple Chutney, peel, core, and chop apples. In a large bowl, combine apples, onion, lemon, bell pepper, ginger, and garlic. In a 2- to 3-quart (1.9- to 2.8-liter) pan, cook vinegar and sugar over high heat, stirring, until sugar has dissolved. Add apple mixture, ground red pepper, and salt. Bring to a boil; reduce heat and simmer, stirring often, until reduced to about 2 cups (470 ml). Let cool. Cover and refrigerate until ready to use or for up to 3 weeks.

Combine honey, sage, garlic, juniper berries, and pepper in a large heavy-duty plastic food bag. Add meat and seal bag securely. Rotate bag to distribute marinade and place in a shallow pan. Refrigerate for at least 2 hours or until next day, turning bag occasionally.

Remove meat from bag, reserving marinade. Set pork in center of cooking grate. Place lid on grill. Cook, brushing once with reserved marinade, until an instant-read thermometer inserted in thickest part of meat registers 160°F/71°C for medium (about 1 hour). Transfer meat to a carving board. Tilt drip pan; skim and discard fat from drippings, reserving drippings.

Slice meat about 1/4 inch (6 mm) thick. Generously coat 6 of the bread slices with mustard. Top with lettuce, meat, and drippings. Add chutney, lettuce, and remaining bread.

MAKES 6 SERVINGS.

Per serving: 570 calories (19% from fat), 12 g total fat (4 g saturated fat), 101 mg cholesterol, 690 mg sodium, 72 g carbohydrates, 6 g fiber, 43 g protein, 124 mg calcium, 4 mg iron

A Word about Fresh Ginger

■ *Buy firm ginger with smooth skin*

■ *To use, cut off and discard exposed ends; peel, then slice thinly, sliver, mince, or grate.*

■ *To store, refrigerate in a plastic bag for up to 2 weeks; do not freeze.*

Pork Satay with Peanut Sauce

Layers of flavor build one upon the other in this Indonesian-inspired recipe with its cumin- and coriander-scented marinade and delicious peanut dipping sauce. Try it with your favorite seasoned rice dish and a refreshing salad of thinly sliced cucumbers dressed with rice vinegar.

Charcoal	Direct
Gas	Indirect/Medium Heat
Marinating time	30 minutes–2 hours
Grilling time	12–15 minutes

	Peanut Sauce (see below)
1	clove garlic
¼	cup (60 ml) soy sauce
1	tablespoon salad oil
1¼	teaspoons *each* ground coriander and ground cumin
1½	pounds (680 g) pork tenderloin, trimmed of fat and silvery membrane, cut into about 24 equal-size slices or pieces
3	tablespoons lemon juice

Peanut Sauce

⅔	cup (160 ml) creamy or crunchy peanut butter
2	cloves garlic, minced or pressed
2	tablespoons firmly packed brown sugar
2	tablespoons *each* lemon juice and soy sauce
¼	teaspoon crushed red pepper flakes

To prepare Peanut Sauce, combine peanut butter, the 2 cloves garlic, and 1 cup (240 ml) water in a 1- to 1½-quart (905-ml to 1.4-liter) pan. Cook over medium heat, stirring, until mixture boils and thickens. Remove from heat and stir in sugar, the 2 tablespoons *each* lemon juice and soy sauce, and red pepper flakes. Let cool. If made ahead, cover and refrigerate until next day; bring to room temperature before serving (thin with water if too thick).

Combine garlic, 2 tablespoons of the soy sauce, oil, and 1 teaspoon each coriander and cumin in a large heavy-duty plastic food bag. Add meat and seal bag securely. Rotate bag to distribute marinade and place in a shallow pan. Refrigerate for at least 30 minutes or up to 2 hours, turning meat occasionally. Meanwhile, combine lemon juice and remaining soy sauce, coriander, and cumin in a small bowl; set aside.

Remove meat from bag and drain, discarding marinade. Thread meat on 6 skewers. Arrange skewers on cooking grate. Place lid on grill. Cook, turning once halfway through cooking time, until pork is no longer pink in center (12 to 15 minutes; cut to test). About 3 minutes before meat is done, brush with lemon juice mixture, using all. Serve with sauce.

MAKES 4 OR 5 SERVINGS.

Per serving: 421 calories (52% from fat), 25 g total fat (5 g saturated fat), 85 mg cholesterol, 1050 mg sodium, 14 g carbohydrates, 2 g fiber, 38 g protein, 31 mg calcium, 3 mg iron

Tame Thai Tenderloin

Here's a Thai pork tenderloin that's mild enough for kids. The sauce is a few notches higher on the heat scale, but it's served on the side so you can add it at your own discretion.

Charcoal	Indirect
Gas	Indirect/Medium Heat
Marinating time	3–6 hours
Grilling time	20–30 minutes

2   pork tenderloins, 12 ounces to 1 pound (340 to 455g) *each*, trimmed of fat and silvery membrane

¾   cup (180 ml) coconut milk

¼   cup (60 ml) soy sauce

2   cloves garlic, minced or pressed

1¼   teaspoons ground coriander

½   teaspoon ground white pepper

¼   teaspoon Oriental red chili paste or liquid hot pepper seasoning

1   tablespoon lemon juice

½   teaspoon sugar

¼   teaspoon ground red pepper (cayenne)

Fold under thin ends of each tenderloin to make piece evenly thick; secure with cotton string. Combine coconut milk, 3 tablespoons of the soy sauce, garlic, 1 teaspoon of the coriander, white pepper, and chili paste in a large heavy-duty plastic food bag. Add meat and seal bag securely. Rotate bag to distribute marinade and place in a shallow pan. Refrigerate for at least 3 hours or up to 6 hours, turning bag occasionally.

Remove meat from bag and drain, discarding marinade. Arrange tenderloins in center of cooking grate. Place lid on grill. Cook until an instant-read thermometer inserted in thickest part of meat (not folded ends) registers 160°F/71°C for medium (20 to 30 minutes). Transfer meat to a carving board and keep warm.

In a small pan, combine lemon juice, remaining soy sauce, remaining coriander, sugar, and ground red pepper. Cook over medium heat, stirring, until hot (about 2 to 3 minutes).

Cut meat across grain into thin, slanting slices. Serve with lemon juice.

MAKES 4 SERVINGS.

Per serving: 351 calories (40% from fat), 17 g total fat (7 g saturated fat), 85 mg cholesterol, 126 mg sodium, 14 g carbohydrates, 1 g fiber, 32 g protein, 62 mg calcium, 3 mg iron

Pork Shoulder Steaks

The simple marinade for these pork shoulder steaks forms a delicious glaze as the meat grills. You might accompany the steaks with a pasta salad made by tossing together a colorful assortment of grilled peppers with your favorite pasta.

Charcoal	Direct
Gas	Indirect/Medium Heat
Marinating time	1 hour or until next day
Grilling time	10–12 minutes

1   beef bouillon cube dissolved in ⅓ cup (80 ml) hot water

1   tablespoon *each* sugar and minced fresh ginger

¼   cup (60 ml) *each* honey and soy sauce

4   pork shoulder steaks, about 2¼ pounds (1.02 kg) *total*, cut ¾ inch (2 cm) thick, trimmed of fat

Very Easy

Combine bouillon mixture, sugar, ginger, honey and soy sauce in a large heavy-duty plastic food bag or nonreactive bowl. Add pork and seal bag (or cover bowl). Rotate bag to distribute marinade and place in a shallow pan. Refrigerate for at least 1 hour or until next day, turning meat occasionally.

Remove steaks from bag and drain, reserving marinade. Arrange steaks on cooking grate. Place lid on grill. Cook, turning once and brushing with reserved marinade halfway through cooking time, until meat near bone is no longer pink (10 to 12 minutes; cut to test).

MAKES 4 SERVINGS.

Per serving: 418 calories (52% from fat), 24 g total fat (8 g saturated fat), 135 mg cholesterol, 1042 mg sodium, 17 g carbohydrates, 0 g fiber, 33 g protein, 11 mg calcium, 2 mg iron

Mixed Sausage Grill with Mustard Cream

Keep an eye out for interesting fresh sausages at the market. Then gather family and friends to sample whatever assortment you find with grilled onions and potatoes and a light mustard cream.

Charcoal	Direct
Gas	Indirect/Medium Heat
Grilling time	28–30 minutes

Mustard Cream (see below)

¼ cup (60 ml) olive oil

2 cloves garlic, minced or pressed

10 russet potatoes, 1½ to 2 inches (3.5 to 5 cm) in diameter, scrubbed

6 onions, about 2½ inches (6 cm) in diameter, cut into quarters

12 assorted fresh sausages, about 3 pounds (1.35 kg) *total,* such as chicken, turkey, Italian, bratwurst, or kielbasa

Mustard Cream

4 egg yolks

2 tablespoons sugar

½ cup (120 ml) Dijon mustard

¼ cup (60 ml) white wine vinegar

2 tablespoons butter or margarine

1 cup (240 ml) whipping cream

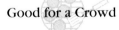

Good for a Crowd

To prepare Mustard Cream, beat egg yolks, sugar, mustard, vinegar, and 1 tablespoon water in top of a double boiler. Add butter. Cook over simmering water, stirring, until mixture coats back of a spoon (5 to 8 minutes). Place top of double boiler in ice water; stir until sauce is cool. In a large bowl, beat whipping cream until stiff peaks form. Gently fold mustard mixture into cream. Cover and refrigerate until ready to use or for up to 3 days.

In a small bowl, combine oil and garlic; set aside. Cut potatoes lengthwise into thirds. Thread onions onto skewers.

Arrange potato slices on cooking grate; brush tops lightly with garlic oil. Place lid on grill. Cook for 10 minutes. Turn, brush with more garlic oil, and arrange onion skewers and sausages directly on potatoes. Cook until potatoes are tender when pierced (about 10 more minutes). Transfer potatoes to a platter and keep warm. Turn sausages and onions, brush onions lightly with remaining garlic oil, and continue to cook until sausages are well browned and no longer pink in center (8 to 10 more minutes; cut to test).

Arrange sausages and onions on platter with potatoes. Serve with mustard sauce.

MAKES 16 SERVINGS.

Per serving: 299 calories (69% from fat), 22 g total fat (9 g saturated fat), 107 mg cholesterol, 625 mg sodium, 12 g carbohydrates, 1 g fiber, 10 g protein, 41 mg calcium, 1 mg iron

FRUITS & VEGETABLES ON THE GRILL

Grilling fresh fruits and vegetables alongside your entrée is a convenient way to add color, flavor, and nutrition to your meals. Try brushing fruits with the basting sauce used on an accompanying entrée, and grill until hot and streaked with brown. For vegetables, prepare them as directed (some require blanching beforehand); butter or baste the vegetables, and grill until hot, tender, and browned.

Grilled Fruits

Charcoal	Indirect
Gas	Indirect/Medium Heat
Grilling time	See chart

About 2 pounds (680 to 905 g) fresh fruit

½ cup (120 ml) butter or margarine, melted; or basting sauce used on accompanying entrée

3 tablespoons firmly packed brown sugar (optional)

1 teaspoon ground cinnamon or ground ginger (optional)

2 tablespoons balsamic vinegar (optional)

Grilled Vegetables

Charcoal	Indirect
Gas	Indirect/Medium Heat
Grilling time	See chart

About 2 pounds (905 g) fresh vegetables

⅓ to ½ cup (80 to 120 ml) olive oil, salad oil, melted butter or margarine, or basting sauce used on accompanying entrée

2 tablespoons chopped fresh thyme, fresh rosemary, fresh oregano, or fresh tarragon; or 2 teaspoons dried thyme, dried rosemary, dried oregano, or dried tarragon (optional)

2 tablespoons balsamic vinegar (optional)

If using small pieces of fruits or vegetables, thread on thin skewers, making sure the pieces lie flat.

Brush prepared fruits or vegetables with butter or basting sauce, and one or more of the optional seasonings, if desired. Arrange fruits or vegetables in center of cooking grate. Place lid on grill. Cook until fruit is hot and streaked with brown or vegetables are streaked with brown and tender when pierced (for grilling times, see charts below and on facing page).

MAKES 6 TO 8 SERVINGS.

Fruit	Preparation	Grilling Time
Apples	Peel, if desired. Cut in half lengthwise; remove cores.	About 30 minutes
Apricots	Cut in half; discard pits. Thread on skewers, making sure fruit lies flat.	4–6 minutes
Bananas	Do not peel. Cut in half lengthwise.	6–8 minutes
Figs	Cut in half lengthwise. Thread on skewers, making sure fruit lies flat.	4–8 minutes
Melons (firm-fleshed types such as cantaloupe)	Cut into wedges 1 to 1½ inches (2.5 to 3.5 cm) wide; discard seeds. Peel, if desired.	8–10 minutes, turning once halfway through cooking time
Nectarines	Cut in half lengthwise; discard pits.	8–10 minutes
Papayas	Peel, if desired. Cut crosswise into rings about ¾ inch (2 cm) thick or cut lengthwise into quarters. Discard seeds.	About 8 minutes
Peaches	Peel and cut in half lengthwise; discard pits.	8–10 minutes
Pears	Peel, if desired. Cut in half lengthwise; remove cores.	8–10 minutes
Pineapple	Peel and core. Cut crosswise into rings about ¾ inch thick or cut lengthwise into wedges about 1 inch (2.5 cm) wide.	8–12 minutes

Vegetable	Preparation	Grilling Time
Artichokes	Trim off stem and coarse outer leaves; cut off top third. Trim thorny tips. Rinse well. Plunge into acidulated water (3 tablespoons vinegar per quart/950 ml water), drain. Cook in boiling water to cover until stem end is tender when pierced (30–45 minutes). Drain; cut in half lengthwise.	10–15 minutes
Asparagus	Snap off tough ends. Cook in simmering water just until tender when pierced (7–10 minutes); drain.	6–8 minutes
Bell peppers	Rinse and pat dry.	About 20 minutes for small and medium-size, about 30 minutes for large; turn occasionally during cooking.
Corn in husks.	Make sure husks enclose cobs completely and are tightly closed at top. Immerse in cold water to cover for about 30 minutes; drain.	30–35 minutes; turn occasionally during cooking.
Corn out of husks	Remove husks and silk. Rinse corn and pat dry.	About 15 minutes; turn occasionally during cooking.
Eggplants	Cut off stem end of Oriental and small regular eggplants. Cut Oriental eggplants in half lenthwise; cut regular eggplants lengthwise into wedges about 1½ inches (3.5 cm) wide.	20–25 minutes; turn once halfway through cooking time.
Fennel	Cut off and discard woody stems. Cut vertically into 4 equal slices.	30–35 minutes
Leeks	Cut off and discard root ends. Trim tops, leaving about 3 inches (8 cm) of green leaves. Discard coarse outer leaves. Split in half lengthwise to within about ½ inch (1 cm) of root ends. Rinse well.	17–20 minutes
Mushrooms (regular or shiitake)	Cut off stem ends.	About 15 minutes
Onions, dry (yellow, white, red)	Do not peel. Cut in half.	30–40 minutes
Onions, green	Trim root ends and top 2 inches (5 cm) of green tops.	6–8 minutes
Potatoes (thin-skinned, russet) sweet potatoes, and yams	Cut small potatoes in half. Cut large ones lengthwise into wedges about 1 inch (2.5 cm) wide. Cook in boiling water to cover until tender when pierced (6–8 minutes).	About 15 minutes; turn once halfway through cooking time.
Radicchio	Cut in half lengthwise.	6–8 minutes
Squash, summer (crookneck, pattypan, zucchini)	Leave small squash whole. Cut longer squash in half lengthwise.	About 15 minutes
Tomatoes	Cut in half.	12–15 minutes

Ballpark Salad

When you gather the gang to watch the game, serve this salad with a pitcher of beer for just the right ambiance. The recipe doubles easily if you're entertaining a crowd.

Charcoal	Direct
Gas	Indirect/Medium Heat
Grilling time	2–4 minutes

¾ cup (180 ml) mayonnaise

2 tablespoons *each* catsup and Dijon mustard

1 pound (455 g) frankfurters or cooked bockwurst sausages

1 head butter lettuce, rinsed and crisped

1 cup (240 ml) diced Swiss cheese

4 hard-cooked eggs, sliced

½ cup (120 ml) *each* chopped dill pickles and sliced celery

1½ cups (360 ml) halved cherry tomatoes

¼ to ½ cup (60 to 120 ml) finely chopped red onion

Good for a Crowd

In a small bowl, combine mayonnaise, catsup, and mustard. If made ahead, cover and refrigerate until next day.

Arrange meat on cooking grate. Place lid on grill. Cook, turning once halfway through cooking time, until meat is browned and hot throughout (2 to 4 minutes).

Slice sausages diagonally ¾ inch (2 cm) thick. On a platter arrange lettuce, cheese, eggs, pickles, celery, tomatoes, and onion to taste in 7 separate rows. Serve with mayonnaise mixture.

MAKES 4 TO 6 SERVINGS.

Per serving: 706 calories (81% from fat), 63 g total fat (19 g saturated fat), 256 mg cholesterol, 1743 mg sodium, 10 g carbohydrates, 1 g fiber, 23 g protein, 266 mg calcium, 2 mg iron

Red Bell Pepper & Sausage Loaf

*This six-person sandwich practically makes itself because of the nifty skewering arrangement.
Two parallel skewers allow you to flip six Italian sausages
and the bell pepper strips all at once.*

Charcoal	Direct
Gas	Indirect/Medium Heat
Grilling time	18–20 minutes

¼ cup (60 ml) butter or margarine, melted

1 clove garlic, minced or pressed

1 long loaf, about 1 pound (455 g), sweet or sourdough French bread, cut in half lengthwise

6 mild Italian sausages, 1¼ to 1½ pounds (565 to 680 g) *total*

2 large red bell peppers, cut into strips about 1½ inches (3.5 cm) wide

6 ounces (170 g) sliced mozzarella, provolone, or jack cheese

Coarse-grained mustard

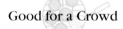

Good for a Crowd

In a small bowl, combine butter and garlic. Brush over cut sides of bread; set aside.

On a metal skewer 12 to 15 inches (30 to 38 cm) long, thread sausages alternately with bell pepper strips, running skewer through end of each sausage and bell pepper strip. Add another skewer parallel to first, running skewer through other end of each sausage and bell pepper strip.

Arrange food on cooking grate. Place lid on grill. Cook, turning once halfway through cooking time, until sausages are well browned and no longer pink in center (18 to 20 minutes; cut to test). About 2 minutes before sausages are done, arrange bread halves, cut side down, on grate. Cook until lightly toasted (about 2 minutes).

Overlap cheese slices on bottom half of bread. Lay sausage and pepper skewer on cheese. Set top half of bread over skewer and, holding firmly in place, pull out skewers. Cut loaf into 6 portions. Serve with mustard.

MAKES 6 SERVINGS.

Per serving: 617 calories (53% from fat), 36 g total fat (16 g saturated fat), 102 mg cholesterol, 1350 mg sodium, 45 g carbohydrates, 3 g fiber, 28 g protein, 230 mg calcium, 3 mg iron

Lamb & Spinach Pockets

Make your weekday dinner special with these sandwiches from the grill. The seasoned lamb patties are filled with olives and eggs and tucked into a pita bread along with spinach and cucumber. The tangy yogurt sauce boasts crunchy bacon pieces and sunflower seeds.

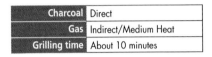

Charcoal	Direct
Gas	Indirect/Medium Heat
Grilling time	About 10 minutes

Yogurt Sauce (see below)

1¼ pounds (565 g) lean ground lamb

½ cup (120 ml) chopped onion

2 tablespoons *each* soy sauce and hot mustard

½ teaspoon *each* celery seeds and dill seeds

2 tablespoons minced parsley

2 hard-cooked medium-size eggs, thinly sliced

1 can, about 2 ounces (55 g), sliced ripe olives

4 pita breads, about 6 inches (15 cm) in diameter

2 cups (470 ml) slivered spinach leaves

1 cup (240 ml) thinly sliced cucumber

Yogurt Sauce

1 cup (240 ml) plain nonfat yogurt

¼ cup (60 ml) crisply cooked, crumbled bacon

2 tablespoons sunflower seeds

In a small bowl, combine ingredients for Yogurt Sauce. Cover and refrigerate until ready to use.

In a large bowl, combine lamb, onion, soy sauce, mustard, celery seeds, dill seeds, and parsley. Shape into 8 thin equal-size patties, each about 4 inches (10 cm) in diameter. Place eggs and olives in center of 4 patties. Top with remaining patties, pinching edges to seal.

Arrange patties on cooking grate. Place lid on grill. Cook, turning once halfway through cooking time (about 10 minutes for medium; cut to test). Fill pita breads with patties, spinach, cucumber, and sauce.

MAKES 4 SERVINGS.

Per serving: 619 calories (44% from fat), 30 g total fat (10 g saturated fat), 194 mg cholesterol, 1337 mg sodium, 45 g carbohydrates, 3 g fiber, 41 g protein, 265 mg calcium, 6 mg iron

Raclette with Vegetables & Sausages

Raclette, a specialty of Switzerland, is traditionally made by melting cheese in front of a fire and serving it with boiled potatoes and tiny pickles. This hearty grilled variation omits the pickles, while adding sausages, carrots, zucchini, and bread.

Charcoal	Direct
Gas	Indirect/Medium Heat
Grilling time	25–30 minutes

1   pound (455 g) *each* carrots and red thin-skinned potatoes, sliced about ¼ inch (6 mm) thick

1   pound (455 g) zucchini, sliced about ½ inch (1 cm) thick

     Salt and pepper

1½   to 2 pounds (680 to 905 g) mellow-flavored cheese, such as Jarlsberg, Swiss, fontina, Gruyère, or jack, trimmed of any wax and cut into chunks

6   to 8 cooked sausages, about 2½ pounds (1.15 kg) *total*, such as knackwurst or kielbasa

1   pound (455 g) sweet or sourdough French bread, sliced

Place carrots, potatoes, and zucchini on separate pieces of heavy-duty foil. Sprinkle each vegetable with salt, pepper, and 2 tablespoons water. Wrap well. Place cheese in a small metal-handled pan; set cheese aside.

Arrange vegetable packets on cooking grate. Place lid on grill. Cook for 20 minutes. Arrange sausages and pan with cheese on grate and continue to cook, turning sausages once halfway through cooking time, until vegetables are tender when pierced, sausages are well browned, and cheese is melted (5 to 10 more minutes).

Transfer vegetables and sausages to individual plates. Arrange bread alongside. Drizzle cheese over all.

MAKES 6 TO 8 SERVINGS.

Per serving: 1158 calories (58% from fat), 74 g total fat (16 g saturated fat), 181 mg cholesterol, 2710 mg sodium, 61 g carbohydrates, 5 g fiber, 58 g protein, 748 mg calcium, 5 mg iron

Spaghetti on the Barbecue

Spaghetti on the barbecue? Actually, it's a great mid-week entertaining idea. Guests make their own spaghetti "to order," with a wonderful assortment of garnishes. Have on hand one small frying pan for every three diners and an adequate supply of hot pads and cooking spoons.

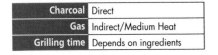

Charcoal	Direct
Gas	Indirect/Medium Heat
Grilling time	Depends on ingredients

1¼ cups (300 ml) extra-virgin, regular, or flavored olive oil

4 large onions, thinly sliced

1 pound (455 g) *each* mild and hot Italian sausages (or all of 1 kind)

1 pound (455 g) small mushrooms, about 1 inch (2.5 cm) in diameter

2 pounds (905 g) dried spaghetti

Garnishes (see below)

Spaghetti sauce or pesto (purchased or homemade), optional

Freshly grated Parmesan cheese

Garnishes

1 pound (455 g) tiny cooked shrimp, rinsed and drained

2 small jars, about 4 ounces (115 g) *each*, chopped pimentos

1 jar, about 6 ounces (170 g), marinated artichokes

2 *each* medium-size zucchini and carrots, finely shredded

2 cups (470 ml) cherry tomatoes, halved

8 green onions, thinly sliced

2 medium-size yellow or green bell peppers, cut into thin slivers

½ cup (120 ml) minced garlic

Heat 1 tablespoon of the oil in a wide frying pan over medium-high heat. Add onions and cook, stirring often, until very soft and golden brown (30 to 40 minutes). Meanwhile, remove casings from sausages. Crumble meat into another wide frying pan. Cook over medium-high heat, stirring often, until meat is well browned (20 to 25 minutes); discard fat. Place onions and meat in separate bowls; set aside. If made ahead, cover and refrigerate for up to 2 days.

Heat 1 more tablespoon oil in either pan over medium heat. Add mushrooms and cook, covered, until juicy (about 5 minutes). Increase heat to medium-high and cook, uncovered, stirring often, until liquid has evaporated and mushrooms are lightly browned (5 to 10 more minutes). Transfer to a bowl and set aside. If made ahead, cover and refrigerate for up to 2 days.

In a 6- to 8-quart (6- to 8-liter) pan, bring 4 quarts (4 liters) water to a boil over high heat. Stir in spaghetti, reduce heat to medium-high, and cook just until tender to bite (about 10 minutes). Drain, pour into a large bowl, and mix with 2 more tablespoons oil; set aside. If made ahead, cover lightly and let stand for up to 4 hours; stir before serving. Place garnishes in bowls.

To serve, place your choice of garnishes in a small metal-handled frying pan; drizzle with oil. Set pan on cooking grate. Place lid on grill. Cook, stirring occasionally, until ingredients are cooked to taste. Add spaghetti and, if desired, sauce, and continue to cook, stirring, until warm. Transfer to an individual plate and sprinkle with cheese to taste. Wipe pan with a paper towel before reusing.

MAKES 8 TO 10 SERVINGS.

Per serving: 232 calories (41% from fat), 8 g total fat (12 g saturated fat), 76 mg cholesterol, 298 mg sodium, 13 g carbohydrates, 0 g fiber, 29 g protein, 57 mg calcium, 8 mg iron

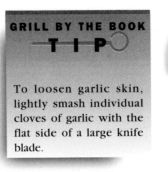

GRILL BY THE BOOK
T I P

To loosen garlic skin, lightly smash individual cloves of garlic with the flat side of a large knife blade.

Pasta with Jerk Pork & Tropical Chutney

Each serving of jerk pork is accompanied by deliciously sauced pasta, slices of fresh papaya, and a chutney that features bananas, lime, and coconut.

Charcoal	Indirect
Gas	Indirect/Medium Heat
Marinating time	20 minutes or until next day
Grilling time	20–30 minutes

Jerk Seasoning (see below)

Tropical Chutney (see below)

2   pork tenderloins, about 12 ounces (340 g) *each*, trimmed of fat and silvery membrane

1   pound (455 g) thin pasta

¾   cup (180 ml) chicken broth

¼   cup (60 ml) seasoned rice wine vinegar

¼   cup (60 ml) minced cilantro

3   tablespoons lime juice

2   teaspoons sugar

2   medium-size papayas, peeled, seeded, and sliced ½ inch (1 cm) thick

    Salt

Jerk Seasoning

¼   cup (60 ml) firmly packed cilantro

3   tablespoons minced fresh ginger

2   tablespoons peppercorns

1   tablespoon *each* ground allspice and brown sugar

2   cloves garlic

¼   teaspoon *each* ground coriander and ground nutmeg

Tropical Chutney

1   large banana, peeled

¾   cup (180 ml) mango chutney

3   tablespoons sweetened flaked coconut

1   tablespoon lime juice

In a blender or food processor, combine ingredients for Jerk Seasoning paste. Add 3 tablespoons water and whirl until smooth. If made ahead, cover and refrigerate for up to 5 days. Meanwhile, coarsely chop and combine ingredients for Tropical Chutney. If made ahead, cover and refrigerate until next day.

Fold under thin ends of tenderloin to make each piece evenly thick; secure with cotton string. Brush meat all over with seasoning paste, wrap airtight, and refrigerate for at least 20 minutes or until next day.

Arrange meat in center of cooking grate. Place lid on grill. Cook until an instant-read thermometer inserted in thickest part of meat (not folded ends) registers 160°F/71°C (25 to 35 minutes). Meanwhile, in a 5- to 6-quart (5- to 6-liter) pan, bring 3 quarts (2.8 liters) water to a boil over high heat. Stir in pasta, reduce heat to medium-high, and cook just until tender to bite (about 4 minutes); drain. Return to pan and add broth. Cook over medium heat, stirring, until most liquid has been absorbed. Stir in vinegar, minced cilantro, lime juice, and sugar. Remove from heat.

Slice pork ½ inch (1 cm) thick. Mound pasta on individual plates. Top with pork and papaya. Serve with chutney. Season to taste with salt.

MAKES 6 SERVINGS.

Per serving: 627 calories (11% from fat), 7 g total fat (3 g saturated fat), 69 mg cholesterol, 743 mg sodium, 106 g carbohydrates, 4 g fiber, 34 g protein, 64 mg calcium, 5 mg iron

Pasta with Grilled Peppers & Italian Sausages

The beauty of this recipe is that the grilling itself can be done ahead of time. Sausages, onions, garlic, and red and yellow peppers come in from the grill to be tossed with pasta and served—hot or at room temperature—when you are ready.

Charcoal	Direct
Gas	Indirect/Medium Heat
Grilling time	18–20 minutes

- 1   pound (455 g) mild Italian sausages
- 1   large red onion, cut into quarters
- 1   *each* large red and yellow bell peppers, cut into quarters
- 1   small head garlic, unpeeled
- 1   pound (455 g) dried penne or ziti
- ¼   cup (60 ml) balsamic or red wine vinegar
- 2   tablespoons Dijon mustard
- 2   teaspoons minced fresh oregano or 1 teaspoon dried oregano
- 1   large tomato, chopped

    Oregano sprigs

Very Easy

Arrange sausages, onion, bell peppers, and garlic head on cooking grate. Place lid on grill. Cook, turning food once halfway through cooking time, until vegetables are soft when pressed and sausages are no longer pink in center (18 to 20 minutes). Meanwhile, bring 3 quarts (2.8 liters) water to a boil over high heat in a 5- to 6-quart (5- to 6-liter) pan. Stir in pasta, reduce heat to medium-high, and cook just until tender to bite (8 to 10 minutes). Drain well and transfer to a large serving bowl.

    Cut garlic in half crosswise. Squeeze pulp into a small bowl and stir in vinegar, mustard, and minced oregano. Slice sausages, onion, and bell peppers. Add to pasta along with garlic mixture and tomato; toss well. Garnish with oregano sprigs. Serve hot or at room temperature.

MAKES 8 SERVINGS.

Per serving: 401 calories (27% from fat), 12 g total fat (4 g saturated fat), 32 mg cholesterol, 487 mg sodium, 55 g carbohydrates, 4 g fiber, 18 g protein, 54 mg calcium, 4 mg iron

RUBS & BASTES FOR POULTRY & FISH

For years cooks have paired assertive rubs and bastes only with beef and other meats of equally robust flavor. When it came to the more delicately flavored poultry and fish, however, they reached for the milder seasonings. Things have changed. Here are some richly flavored seasoning mixtures that will enhance all kinds of poultry and fish entrées. For rubs and bastes for meats, see pages 22–23.

Salt & Herb Rub

1   tablespoon *each* minced fresh oregano, fresh rosemary, and fresh thyme

2   teaspoons coarse salt

1½ teaspoons freshly ground pepper

2   tablespoons lemon juice

In a small bowl, combine oregano, rosemary, thyme, salt, and pepper. Brush chicken or fish with lemon juice; pat herb mixture all over food before cooking.

MAKES ABOUT ¼ CUP (60 ML), ENOUGH FOR ABOUT 4 SERVINGS OF POULTRY OR FISH.

Per serving: 6 calories (12% from fat), 0 g total fat (0 g saturated fat), 0 mg cholesterol, 739 mg sodium, 1 g carbohydrates, 0 g fiber, 0 g protein, 21 mg calcium, 0 mg iron

Soy Sauce Baste

½   cup (120 ml) rice wine vinegar or white wine vinegar

¼   cup (60 ml) soy sauce

1   tablespoon Oriental sesame oil

2   teaspoons sugar

1   clove garlic

1   tablespoon minced fresh ginger (optional)

In a small bowl, combine vinegar, soy sauce, oil, sugar, garlic, and, if desired, ginger. Brush mixture all over poultry or fish while it cooks.

MAKES ABOUT 1 CUP (180 TO 240 ML), ENOUGH FOR ABOUT 8 SERVINGS OF POULTRY OR FISH.

Per serving: 26 calories (57% from fat), 2 g total fat (0 g saturated fat), 0 mg cholesterol, 514 mg sodium, 2 g carbohydrates, 0 g fiber, 0 g protein, 2 mg calcium, 0 mg iron

Fragrant Oils for Basting

1   tablespoon *each* olive oil, soy sauce, and rice wine vinegar

1   teaspoon *each* chili oil and Oriental sesame oil

    Lemon wedges

In a small bowl, combine olive oil, soy sauce, vinegar, chili oil, and sesame oil. Brush oil mixture all over poultry or fish before cooking. Serve lemon wedges to squeeze over hot cooked food.

MAKES ABOUT ¼ CUP (60 ML), ENOUGH FOR 3 OR 4 SERVINGS OF POULTRY OR FISH.

Per serving: 53 calories (94% from fat), 6 g total fat (1 g saturated fat), 0 mg cholesterol, 257 mg sodium, 1 g carbohydrates, 0 g fiber, 0 g protein, 1 mg calcium, 0 mg iron

Quick Hoisin Baste

½   cup (120 ml) hoisin or plum sauce

2   tablespoons *each* soy sauce and white wine vinegar

In a small bowl, combine hoisin, soy sauce, and vinegar. Brush hoisin mixture all over poultry or fish while it cooks.

MAKES ¾ CUP (180 ML), ENOUGH FOR 10 TO 12 SERVINGS OF POULTRY OR FISH.

Per serving: 35 calories (0% from fat), 0 g total fat (0 g saturated fat), 0 mg cholesterol, 416 mg sodium, 7 g carbohydrates, 0 g fiber, 0g protein, 1 mg calcium, 0 mg iron

Tarragon-Dijon Chicken Breasts in Foil

Small potatoes grill together with mustard-marinated chicken breasts in one foil bundle, a convenient and delicious way to prepare a meal. If you like, parboil small artichokes, cut them in half, and add them to the packet.

Charcoal	Indirect
Gas	Indirect/Medium Heat
Marinating time	1 hour or until next day
Grilling time	35–45 minutes

6   chicken breast halves, about 3 pounds (1.35 kg) *total*, skinned

¼   cup (60 ml) Dijon mustard

¼   cup (60 ml) tarragon vinegar or white wine vinegar

2   tablespoons olive oil

4   teaspoons minced fresh tarragon or 2 teaspoons dried tarragon

¼   teaspoon freshly ground pepper

12   to 15 small thin-skinned potatoes, 1 to 1½ inches (2.5 to 3.5 cm) in diameter, scrubbed

      Salt

Lowfat

Rinse chicken and pat dry. Combine mustard, vinegar, oil, tarragon, and pepper in a large heavy-duty plastic food bag or nonreactive bowl. Add chicken and seal bag (or cover bowl). Rotate bag to distribute marinade and place in a shallow pan. Refrigerate for at least 1 hour or until next day, turning chicken occasionally.

Remove chicken from bag and drain, reserving marinade. Arrange chicken in center of an 18- by 30-inch (46- by 75-cm) piece of heavy-duty foil; pile potatoes over chicken. Spoon reserved marinade over potatoes. Bring foil edges up over potatoes and crimp well to seal.

Set foil bundle in center of cooking grate. Place lid on grill. Cook until chicken near bone is no longer pink and potatoes are tender when pierced (35 to 45 minutes; cut chicken to test). Transfer bundle to a platter and open foil to serve. Season to taste with salt.

MAKES 4 OR 5 SERVINGS.

Per serving: 411 calories (20% from fat), 8 g total fat (1 g saturated fat), 129 mg cholesterol, 443 mg sodium, 24 g carbohydrates, 2 g fiber, 54 g protein, 36 mg calcium, 3 mg iron

Chicken with Bay, Squash & Cherry Tomatoes

In this dish, every ingredient is cooked to perfection because it is grilled on its own separate skewer. The bay leaves give the skewers an attractive appearance and a wonderful aroma.

Charcoal	Indirect
Gas	Indirect/Medium Heat
Marinating time	6 hours or until next day
Grilling time	35–45 minutes

12 chicken thighs, about
    4 pounds (1.8 kg) *total*

3   tablespoons *each* Dijon
    mustard and white wine
    vinegar

½   cup (120 ml) olive oil
    or salad oil

1   teaspoon coarsely ground
    pepper

    About 36 fresh bay leaves;
    or 36 dried bay leaves
    soaked in hot water
    for 1 hour

4   medium-size crookneck
    squash, sliced about ½ inch
    (1 cm) thick

3   cups (710 ml) cherry
    tomatoes

Skin chicken, if desired; rinse and pat dry. Combine mustard, vinegar, oil, and pepper in a large heavy-duty plastic food bag. Add chicken, tucking 6 of the bay leaves between pieces. Seal bag securely. Rotate bag to distribute marinade and place in a shallow pan. Refrigerate for at least 6 hours or until next day, turning chicken occasionally.

Remove chicken from bag and drain, reserving marinade. Add squash to reserved marinade; turn to coat. Remove squash and bay leaves from bag, discarding marinade.

On each of 3 metal skewers 12 to 15 inches (30 to 38 cm) long, alternate 4 chicken thighs with 4 bay leaves (including those from marinade). On each of 3 more skewers, thread 4 bay leaves with 6 or 8 squash slices, piercing through skin on sides of slices. On each of 3 more skewers, thread a third of the tomatoes with 4 bay leaves.

Arrange chicken skewers in center of cooking grate. Place lid on grill. Cook for 20 minutes. Arrange squash skewers on cooking grate. Continue to cook, turning squash once halfway through cooking time, until squash is soft when pressed and meat near thighbone is no longer pink (15 to 25 more minutes; cut chicken to test). About 5 minutes before chicken is done, arrange tomato skewers on cooking grate and cook, turning once, until hot (about 5 minutes).

MAKES 6 SERVINGS.

Per serving: 515 calories (60% from fat), 34 g total fat (8 g saturated fat), 146 mg cholesterol, 228 mg sodium, 10 g carbohydrates, 1 g fiber, 41 g protein, 92 mg calcium, 5 mg iron

GRILL BY THE BOOK
T I P

Bay leaves add flavor and aroma to cooked dishes and make a colorful presentation. However, their spines can be sharp as needles: DO NOT EAT THEM.

Taco Bowl Salad with Grilled Chicken

Baked tortilla bowls are a smashing way to present these main-course salads. To make the bowls, drape moistened tortillas over an empty can and bake until crisp. Alternatively, you can present the salad on flat tortillas like a tostada.

Charcoal	Direct
Gas	Indirect/Medium Heat
Marinating time	1 hour or until next day
Grilling time	About 10 minutes

Citrus Marinade (see below)

6   skinless, boneless chicken breast halves, about 5 ounces (140 g) *each*

1   large red onion, sliced crosswise about ½ inch (1 cm) thick

1½   teaspoons salad oil

6   large flour tortillas, 10 to 13 inches (25 to 33 cm) in diameter

2   cans black beans, about 15 ounces (425 g) *each*, rinsed and drained

1   medium-size red bell pepper, chopped

3   quarts (2.8 liters) finely shredded iceberg lettuce

1   large avocado, peeled, pitted, and sliced

Cilantro sprigs

Sour cream

Citrus Marinade

1½   cups (360 ml) orange juice

1¼   cups (300 ml) lime juice

⅓   cup (80 ml) minced shallots

1¾   teaspoons sugar

½   cup (120 ml) chopped cilantro

1½   teaspoons *each* crushed red pepper flakes and crushed cumin seeds

2   cloves garlic, minced or pressed

In a large bowl, combine ingredients for Citrus Marinade. Rinse chicken and pat dry. Place chicken and onion in separate large heavy-duty plastic food bags. Pour ⅓ cup (80 ml) of the marinade into each bag and seal securely. Rotate bags to distribute marinade and place in a shallow pan. Refrigerate for at least 1 hour or until next day, turning bags occasionally.

Meanwhile, for each tortilla, set 1 empty food can, about 4 inches (10 cm) in diameter, on a foil-lined baking sheet. Cover with foil. Pour ¼ teaspoon of the oil into a pan with ½ inch (1 cm) water. Quickly dip tortilla in water; remove, drain, and drape over can. Bake in a 450°F (230°C) oven until tortilla is firm (4 to 5 minutes). Lift off can and place, cup side up, on baking sheet (if sides sag, brace with crumpled foil). Bake until crisp (2 to 3 more minutes). Repeat for remaining tortillas or bake several at once.

Drain marinade from onion into a glass measure; add remaining marinade to make ½ cup (120 ml). Combine in bowl with beans and bell pepper; set aside. Remove chicken from bag and drain, discarding marinade. Arrange chicken and onion on cooking grate. Place lid on grill. Cook, turning once halfway through cooking time, until meat in thickest part is no longer pink (about 10 minutes; cut chicken to test). Slice chicken; separate onion into rings. Layer lettuce, bean salad, chicken, onion, and avocado in tortilla bowls. Garnish with cilantro sprigs. Serve with sour cream and remaining marinade.

MAKES 6 SERVINGS.

Per serving: 659 calories (21% from fat), 15 g total fat (2 g saturated fat), 82 mg cholesterol, 728 mg sodium, 83 g carbohydrates, 10 g fiber, 49 g protein, 263 mg calcium, 8 mg iron

Turkey on Sesame Bun

Here's a tasty, simple meal that takes no more than 10 minutes to prepare. Slices of grilled turkey breast are served on toasted buns with lettuce and a lemon-herb mayonnaise.

Charcoal	Direct
Gas	Indirect/Medium Heat
Grilling time	3–5 minutes

Lemon-Herb Mayonnaise (see below)

1¼ to 1½ pounds (565 to 680 g) skinless, boneless turkey breast slices, cut about ¼ inch (6 mm) thick

3 tablespoons olive oil

2 tablespoons lemon juice

6 large butter lettuce leaves, rinsed and crisped

1 large tomato, cut crosswise into 6 slices

6 sliced sesame sandwich or hamburger buns, toasted

Salt and pepper

Lemon-Herb Mayonnaise

½ cup (120 ml) mayonnaise

1 tablespoon minced fresh marjoram or 1 teaspoon dried marjoram

½ teaspoon grated lemon zest

2 teaspoons lemon juice

Very Easy

In a small bowl, combine ingredients for Lemon-Herb Mayonnaise. Cover and refrigerate until ready to use or until next day.

Brush turkey all over with oil and lemon juice. Arrange turkey slices on cooking grate. Place lid on grill. Cook, turning once halfway through cooking time, until meat in center is no longer pink (3 to 5 minutes; cut to test).

Place lettuce, turkey, and tomato slices on buns. Top with Lemon-Herb Mayonnaise. Season to taste with salt and pepper.

MAKES 6 SERVINGS.

Per serving: 446 calories (50% from fat), 24 g total fat (4 g saturated fat), 76 mg cholesterol, 404 mg sodium, 26 g carbohydrates, 2 g fiber, 30 g protein, 79 mg calcium, 3 g iron

Turkey Club with Tomato Chutney

All the good flavors of a club sandwich can be found in this breadless version. Tomato chutney and lettuce are rolled in pounded turkey breast; then the rolls are wrapped with pancetta or bacon. You can prepare the rolls ahead of time and pop them on the grill just before dinner.

Charcoal	Direct
Gas	Indirect/Medium Heat
Grilling time	10–15 minutes

Tomato Chutney (see below)

8 skinless, boneless turkey breast slices or cutlets, 2 to 3 ounces (55 to 85 g) *each,* cut about ⅜ inch (9 mm) thick

2 tablespoons mayonnaise

1 tablespoon coarse-grained Dijon mustard

2 cups (470 ml) shredded romaine lettuce

16 thin slices pancetta or 8 slices bacon, 6 to 7 ounces (170 to 200 g) *total*

Tomato Chutney

1½ pounds (680 g) pear-shaped (Roma-type) tomatoes, chopped

⅔ cup (160 ml) minced shallots

2 tablespoons minced fresh ginger

⅔ cup (135 g) sugar

⅓ cup (80 ml) apple cider vinegar

¼ teaspoon crushed red pepper flakes

In a 2- to 3-quart (1.9- to 2.8-liter) pan, combine ingredients for Tomato Chutney. Boil over high heat, stirring often, until reduced to about 2 cups/470 ml (45 to 55 minutes). Set aside. If made ahead, let cool; then cover and refrigerate for up to 3 weeks.

Rinse turkey and pat dry. With a flat-surfaced mallet, pound each slice between sheets of plastic wrap until about ⅛ inch (3 mm) thick. In a small bowl, combine mayonnaise and mustard. Spread evenly over turkey slices. Mound lettuce in center of turkey and top each turkey slice with 1 tablespoon of the chutney. Roll to enclose filling. Wrap 2 slices pancetta (or 1 slice bacon) around each roll. (At this point, you may cover and refrigerate until next day.)

Arrange turkey rolls on cooking grate. Place lid on grill. Cook, turning once halfway through cooking time, until meat in center is no longer pink (10 to 15 minutes; cut to test). Serve with remaining chutney.

Makes 4 to 6 servings.

Per serving: 382 calories (22% from fat), 9 g total fat (2 g saturated fat), 87 mg cholesterol, 518 mg sodium, 39 g carbohydrates, 2 g fiber, 35 g protein, 39 mg calcium, 3 mg iron

GRILLED BREADS

Breads on the barbecue? Why not! You'll be amazed at the delicious results, whether you're adding seasonings to a loaf that's ready to bake or making polenta from scratch. Enjoy either of the breads featured on this page as a first course with cheese and salad or as an accompaniment with grilled meats, fish, or chicken.

Grilled Italian Flat Bread

Charcoal	Indirect
Gas	Indirect/Medium Heat
	5–7 minutes

1 loaf, about 1 pound (455 g), frozen whole wheat or white bread dough, thawed

About ¼ cup (60 ml) olive oil

⅓ cup (80 ml) chopped fresh basil or 1 tablespoon dried basil

¼ cup (60 ml) chopped fresh oregano or 2 teaspoons dried oregano

¼ cup (60 ml) minced parsley

Kosher or regular salt

Divide bread dough in half. Working with 1 piece at a time (cover other piece), roll on a floured board into a round about 10 inches (25 cm) wide. Drizzle with 1 tablespoon of the oil. Sprinkle with a quarter of the basil, oregano, and parsley. Sprinkle with salt. Use rolling pin to lightly press in seasonings.

Turn round over onto a piece of floured foil; repeat seasoning and rolling. Place foil-supported round on a 12- by 15-inch (30- by 38-cm) baking sheet. Repeat for remaining dough.

Supporting dough with foil, flip a round of dough onto center of cooking grate; peel off foil.

Place lid on grill. Cook, turning once halfway through cooking time, until bread is speckled with gold on both sides (5 to 7 minutes). Using a wide metal spatula, remove bread from grill. Repeat for remaining round.

MAKES 2 ROUNDS (2 OR 3 SERVINGS PER ROUND).

Per serving: 305 calories (37% from fat), 13 g total fat (1 g saturated fat), 0 mg cholesterol, 529 mg sodium, 41 g carbohydrates, 2 g fiber, 7 g protein, 227 mg calcium, 5 mg iron

Grilled Polenta

Charcoal	Indirect
Gas	Indirect/Medium Heat
Grilling time	8–10 minutes

3 tablespoons oil from oil-packed dried tomatoes or olive oil

1 small onion, finely chopped

3 tablespoons *each* minced green bell pepper and drained oil-packed dried tomatoes

3 cloves garlic, minced or pressed

4½ cups (1 liter) chicken broth

1½ cups (360 ml) polenta or yellow cornmeal

Slivered oil-packed dried tomatoes

Shredded Parmesan cheese (optional)

Heat 2 tablespoons of the oil in a 4- to 5-quart (4- to 5-liter) pan over medium heat. Add onion, bell pepper, minced dried tomatoes, and garlic. Cook, stirring occasionally, until onions are soft (about 7 minutes). Add 3 cups (710 ml) of the broth and bring to a boil over high heat. Meanwhile, combine polenta and remaining broth in a small bowl.

Using a long-handled spoon, gradually stir polenta mixture into hot broth. Reduce heat and cook, stirring, for 5 more minutes. Remove from heat and at once spoon polenta into a 4- by 8-inch (10- by 20-cm) foil loaf pan. Let stand for about 30 minutes.

Run a knife around pan and turn polenta out onto a board. Cut crosswise into 8 slices; cut slices diagonally in half. Lightly brush with remaining oil. Arrange slices in center of cooking grate. Place lid on grill. Cook until hot (8 to 10 minutes). Using a metal spatula, remove from grill. Top with slivered dried tomatoes and cheese.

MAKES 8 SERVINGS.

Per serving: 194 calories (44% from fat), 9 g total fat (1 g saturated fat), 0 mg cholesterol, 566 mg sodium, 23 g carbohydrates, 2 g fiber, 4 g protein, 9 mg calcium, 1 mg iron

Fish & Vegetable Skewers

These colorful vegetable-laden skewers are low in fat. All you need to go with them is some freshly cooked rice or orzo.

Charcoal	Direct
Gas	Indirect/Medium Heat
Marinating time	3 hours or until next day
Grilling time	About 10 minutes

About 1½ pounds (680 g) skinless, boneless firm-textured fish steaks, such as swordfish, halibut, shark, or lingcod, cut about 1 inch (2.5 cm) thick

¼   cup (60 ml) olive oil

½   cup (120 ml) lemon juice

2   tablespoons minced fresh ginger

1   clove garlic, minced or pressed

1   teaspoon soy sauce

¼   teaspoon pepper

2   small zucchini, sliced about ¼ inch (6 mm) thick

1   large red onion, cut into about 1-inch (2.5-cm) chunks

2   *each* large red and yellow bell peppers, cut into about 1-inch (2.5-cm) squares

12   to 18 large mushrooms

Salt

Rinse fish and pat dry. Cut into about 1-inch (2.5-cm) cubes.

Combine oil, lemon juice, ginger, garlic, soy sauce, and pepper in a large heavy-duty plastic food bag or nonreactive bowl. Add fish and seal bag (or cover bowl). Rotate bag to distribute marinade and set in a shallow pan. Refrigerate for at least 3 hours or until next day, turning fish occasionally.

Add zucchini, onion, bell peppers, and mushrooms to bag, turning to coat vegetables with marinade. Remove fish and vegetables from bag and drain, discarding marinade. Thread alternately on 6 skewers at least 12 inches (30 cm) long.

Arrange skewers on cooking grate. Place lid on grill. Cook, turning once halfway through cooking time, until fish is opaque but still moist in center (about 10 minutes; cut to test). Season to taste with salt.

MAKES 4 TO 6 SERVINGS.

Per serving: 334 calories (34% from fat), 13 g total fat (3 g saturated fat), 62 mg cholesterol, 194 mg sodium, 20 g carbohydrates, 4 g fiber, 36 g protein, 50 mg calcium, 4 mg iron

Niçoise Sandwich with Caper Aioli

Here's a tuna sandwich with a difference—no can to open. If you can't find fresh tuna in your regular market, try a Japanese market. Depending on the season and your location, you may find such varieties as yellowfin (ahi), bluefin, albacore, tombo, or skipjack.

Charcoal	Direct
Gas	Indirect/Medium Heat
Grilling time	About 10 minutes

Caper Aioli (see below)

4   tuna steaks, about 4 ounces (115 g) *each,* cut about 1 inch (2.5 cm) thick

1   tablespoon olive oil or salad oil

½   baguette, about 1-pound (455-g) size, about 3 inches (8 cm) in diameter

1   medium-size tomato, sliced

8   canned anchovy fillets

4   large butter lettuce leaves, rinsed and crisped

2   cups (470 ml) yellow or red bell pepper strips

2   cups (470 ml) *each* cold cooked green beans and cold boiled tiny red thin-skinned potatoes

½   cup (120 ml) Niçoise olives (optional)

Caper Aioli

⅔   cup (160 ml) mayonnaise

2   cloves garlic, minced or pressed

1   tablespoon *each* drained minced capers and lemon juice

In a small bowl, combine ingredients for Caper Aioli. Cover and refrigerate until ready to use or for up to 5 days.

Rinse fish and pat dry. Brush all over with oil. Arrange fish on cooking grate. Place lid on grill. Cook, turning once with a wide metal spatula halfway through cooking time, until fish is opaque but still moist in center (about 10 minutes; cut to test).

Cut baguette crosswise into 4 equal pieces; split each almost in half horizontally. Spread some of the aioli on bread. Add tomato slices, tuna, and anchovies. Place sandwiches on individual plates; arrange lettuce, bell peppers, beans, potatoes, and, if desired, olives alongside. Serve with remaining aioli.

MAKES 4 SERVINGS.

Per serving: 745 calories (49% from fat), 41 g total fat (7 g saturated fat), 69 mg cholesterol, 960 mg sodium, 57 g carbohydrates, 5 g fiber, 38 g protein, 112 mg calcium, 5 mg iron

Fish Tacos with Cilantro Slaw

If you like cilantro, you'll love this cabbage slaw laden with the stuff. The slaw makes a fine partner for tequila-laced fish tacos with their salsa, guacamole, and sour cream.

Charcoal	Direct
Gas	Indirect/Medium Heat
Marinating time	15 minutes–4 hours
Grilling time	10–20 minutes

1¾ to 2 pounds (795 to 905 g) firm-textured white-fleshed fish fillets or steaks, such as Chilean sea bass, swordfish, or sturgeon, cut 1 to 1¼ inches (2.5 to 3 cm) thick

⅓ cup (80 ml) lime juice

3 tablespoons tequila (optional)

Cilantro Slaw (see below)

6 to 12 flour tortillas, about 7 inches (18 cm) in diameter, or corn tortillas, about 6 inches (15 cm) in diameter

About 1 cup (240 ml) *each* salsa and guacamole (purchased or homemade)

Sour cream or plain nonfat yogurt

Cilantro Slaw

3 cups (710 ml) *each* finely shredded green and red cabbages

1 cup (240 ml) firmly packed cilantro leaves, minced

¼ cup (60 ml) lime juice

1 tablespoon salad oil

½ teaspoon cumin seeds

1 teaspoon sugar

Salt and pepper

Rinse fish and pat dry. Place in a large heavy-duty plastic food bag or nonreactive bowl. Pour in lime juice and, if desired, tequila. Seal bag (or cover bowl). Rotate bag to distribute marinade and place in a shallow pan. Refrigerate for at least 15 minutes or up to 4 hours, turning fish occasionally.

Meanwhile, to prepare Cilantro Slaw, combine green cabbage, red cabbage, cilantro, lime juice, oil, cumin seeds, and sugar in a large bowl. Season to taste with salt and pepper. Cover and refrigerate until ready to use or for up to 4 hours.

Lightly dampen tortillas, stack, and wrap in heavy-duty foil. Remove fish from bag and drain, discarding marinade. Arrange fish and tortillas on cooking grate. Place lid on grill. Cook, turning fish and tortillas once halfway through cooking time, until fish is opaque but still moist in thickest part (10 to 12 minutes; cut to test).

Transfer fish to a platter. Cut in chunks (removing any bones and skin) and place in tortillas. Add slaw, salsa, guacamole, and sour cream to taste. Fold to enclose.

MAKES 6 SERVINGS.

Per serving: 455 calories (33% from fat), 17 g total fat (3 g saturated fat), 58 mg cholesterol, 1054 mg sodium, 43 g carbohydrates, 4 g fiber, 33 g protein, 131 mg calcium, 3 mg iron

GRILL BY THE BOOK
T I P

To warm tortillas, lightly sprinkle them with water, wrap them in foil, and heat them on the grill, turning once, for about 10 minutes

Individual Pizzas on the Grill

Let the kids choose and assemble their favorite topping for these single-serving pizzas. Instead of using frozen bread dough, you can substitute the small prebaked rounds of Italian bread sold in many large supermarkets.

Charcoal	Direct
Gas	Indirect/Medium Heat
Grilling time	5–7 minutes

1 loaf, about 1 pound (455 g), frozen white or whole wheat bread dough, thawed

About 2 tablespoons olive oil

Topping of your choice (see facing page)

Nectarine, Basil & Parmesan Pizza

On a floured board, divide dough into 4 equal-size pieces; shape into balls. Roll each into a round 5 to 6 inches (12.5 to 15 cm) in diameter. Brush tops with oil and place each, oiled side down, on a piece of foil about 12 by 18 inches (30 by 46 cm). Brush other side with oil. With your hands, flatten rounds to about ⅛ inch (3 mm) thick and 7 to 8 inches (18 to 20 cm) in diameter. Let stand, uncovered, at room temperature until slightly puffy (20 to 30 minutes).

Keeping dough on foil, transport rounds in a single layer on 2 large baking sheets. Using foil, flip dough over onto cooking grate, placing rounds slightly apart. Place lid on grill. Cook until golden brown on bottom (2 to 3 minutes).

Using a wide metal spatula, transfer rounds, browned side up, to baking sheets. Prepare and apply toppings of your choice. Slide pizzas from baking sheets onto cooking grate. Place lid on grill. Cook until toppings are hot and bottom of bread is crisp and flecked with brown (3 to 5 more minutes).

MAKES 4 SERVINGS.

Per serving: 406 calories (33% from fat), 15 g total fat (3 g saturated fat), 12 mg cholesterol, 766 mg sodium, 55 g carbohydrates, 3 g fiber, 13 g protein, 361 mg calcium, 5 mg iron

Nectarine, Basil & Parmesan Topping

1	small nectarine, pitted
½	teaspoon balsamic or seasoned rice vinegar
1	teaspoon extra-virgin olive oil
⅓	cup (80 ml) shredded jack cheese
2	tablespoons shaved Parmesan cheese
1	tablespoon pine nuts
2	tablespoons finely shredded fresh basil or ½ teaspoon dried basil

Thinly slice nectarine into a small bowl and mix with vinegar and oil. Top 1 bread round with jack and Parmesan cheeses. With a slotted spoon, scatter nectarine over top. Sprinkle with pine nuts. Follow directions for grilling pizza. Just before serving, sprinkle with basil.

MAKES 1 SERVING.

Per serving: 164 calories (45% from fat), 8 g total fat (3 g saturated fat), 12 mg cholesterol, 272 mg sodium, 16 g carbohydrates, 1 g fiber, 7 g protein, 178 mg calcium, 2 mg iron

Vegetarian

Charcoal	Direct
Gas	Indirect/Medium Heat
Grilling time	3–5 minutes

1	large pear-shaped (Roma-type) tomato
2	tablespoons pesto (purchased or homemade)
½	cup (120 ml) shredded mozzarella cheese

Tomato & Pesto Topping

Slice tomato lengthwise ½ inch (1 cm) thick. Arrange slices on cooking grate. Place lid on grill. Cook, turning once halfway through cooking time, until browned on both sides (3 to 5 minutes). Spread 1 bread round with pesto; top with tomato slices and cheese. Follow directions for grilling pizza.

MAKES 1 SERVING.

Per serving: 407 calories (49% from fat), 16 g total fat (11 g saturated fat), 12 mg cholesterol, 769 mg sodium, 54 g carbohydrates, 2 g fiber, 13 g protein, 337 mg calcium, 7 mg iron

Vegetarian

1	tablespoon pizza sauce (purchased or homemade)
	Red and green bell pepper strips
2	or 3 yellow or red cherry tomatoes, halved
1	large mushroom, sliced
2	ripe olives, quartered
2	tablespoons shredded mozzarella cheese

Mixed Vegetable Topping

Spread pizza sauce on 1 bread round. Top with bell peppers, tomatoes, mushroom, olives, and cheese. Follow directions for grilling pizza.

MAKES 1 SERVING.

Per serving: 392 calories (31% from fat), 13 g total fat (3 g saturated fat), 11 mg cholesterol, 845 mg sodium, 56 g carbohydrates, 3 g fiber, 13 g protein, 326 mg calcium, 6 mg iron

Vegetarian

Grilled Vegetables on Cornbread

Cornbread climbs to a new league when it's cut into triangles, toasted on the grill, and topped with a savory vegetable and cheese combination. You can substitute cooked polenta (coarsely ground cornmeal) for the cornbread, if you like. Try the recipe on page 55.

Charcoal	Direct
Gas	Indirect/Medium Heat
Grilling time	13–20 minutes

4   small leeks

1   small eggplant

1   tablespoon olive oil

Sun-dried Tomato Relish (see below)

1   baked cornbread, about 8 inches (20 cm) square

8   ounces (230 g) fontina cheese, shredded

Sun-Dried Tomato Relish

3   tablespoons olive oil

2   tablespoons balsamic or red wine vinegar

2   tablespoons *each* Greek-style olives and drained minced sun-dried tomatoes packed in oil

1   tablespoon minced fresh rosemary or 1 teaspoon crumbled dried rosemary

1   clove garlic, minced or pressed

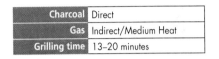

Vegetarian

Cut off and discard root ends from leeks. Trim tops, leaving about 3 inches (8 cm) of green leaves. Discard coarse outer leaves. Split leeks in half lengthwise and rinse well to remove any dirt; drain. Cut in half, if desired. Cut eggplant lengthwise into 8 wedges. Brush vegetables all over with the 1 tablespoon oil.

Arrange leeks and eggplant on cooking grate. Place lid on grill. Cook, turning once halfway through cooking time, until vegetables are browned and eggplant is very soft when pressed (8 to 10 minutes for leeks; 10 to 15 minutes for eggplant). If made ahead, cover vegetables and let stand for up to 6 hours. Meanwhile, combine ingredients for Sun-dried Tomato Relish in a small bowl; set aside.

Cut cornbread into 4 triangles and split horizontally. Lay cornbread, cut side up, on a large baking sheet. Arrange eggplant and leeks on cornbread; top with cheese and relish. Set baking sheet on cooking grate. Place lid on grill. Cook until cheese is melted (about 5 minutes). Using a wide metal spatula, arrange 2 triangles on each of 4 individual plates.

MAKES 4 SERVINGS.

Per serving: 740 calories (55% from fat), 46 g total fat (16 g saturated fat), 121 mg cholesterol, 1317 mg sodium, 61 g carbohydrates, 6 g fiber, 23 g protein, 456 mg calcium, 4 mg iron

GRILL BY THE BOOK
T I P

Go Italian: substitute a slice of grilled polenta (see page 55) for the cornbread.

Index